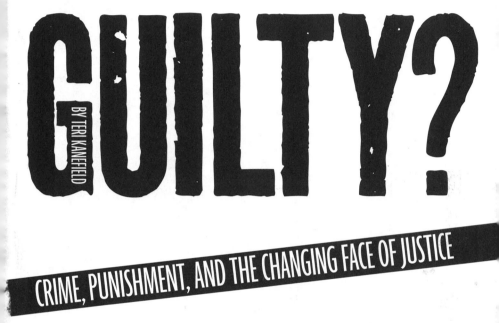

GUILTY?

BY TERI KANEFIELD

CRIME, PUNISHMENT, AND THE CHANGING FACE OF JUSTICE

HOUGHTON MIFFLIN HARCOURT

Boston   New York

www.hmhco.com

Library of Congress Cataloging-in-Publication Data
Kanefield, Teri, 1960– author.

Guilty : crime, punishment, and the changing face of criminal justice / by Teri Kanefield.

p. cm.

ISBN 978-0-544-14896-3

1. Criminal justice, Administration of—United States—Juvenile literature.
2. Guilt (Law)—United States—Juvenile literature.
3. Judicial process—United States—Juvenile literature. I. Title.

KF9223.K29 2014

364.973—dc23

2013042010

Printed in the U.S.A.

DOC 10 9 8 7 6 5 4 3 2 1

4500502181

For Andy

CONTENTS

INTRODUCTION

"That ought to be a crime!"
"People should not be allowed to get away with that behavior!"
"We need to be tougher on crime!"
"Police officers need to get criminals off the streets so law-abiding citizens can live in peace."

Statements like these, often heard on television and elsewhere, represent the *crime control* model of criminal law. Under this model, law and order is the ideal. Preventing crime is the most important function of criminal law, because— according to this theory—without law and order, you cannot have a free society and people cannot feel secure.

The crime control model values well-trained and efficient police squads that know how to investigate a crime scene, preserve evidence, question suspects, and efficiently figure out who most likely committed the crime so the culprit can be brought to justice. The crime control model is based on the assumption that crimes are committed by bad people who belong in jail, which in turn is based on the belief that criminal laws represent absolute standards of right and wrong.

The crime control model is one with which almost everyone is familiar, and with which many people feel comfortable. But this doesn't mean the crime control model doesn't have problems and flaws. For example, ideas about what should be criminalized spring from ever-changing cultural beliefs, and thus change over time and across cultures. If reasonable people can disagree about what behavior to criminalize, how can we be sure that the behavior we are criminalizing is morally wrong? Or that the behavior we are not criminalizing is morally acceptable?

If defining crimes presents moral dilemmas, deciding when and how a government should inflict punishment presents even more difficult moral questions.

There is another model of criminal law: the due process model, which values individual liberty above crime control. Many of those who favor the due process model agree that there are dangerous people out there who need to be stopped, but they also believe that being too tough on crime causes more problems than it solves. The due process model embraces the idea that it is better for a guilty person to walk free than an innocent person to be put in jail—so the due process model makes it more difficult for citizens to be arrested, tried, and punished.

Critics of the due process model point out that people should be accountable for their behavior and a system that might allow a guilty person to walk free is deeply flawed.

The two models offer different ways to think about the issues.

For some, the ideal system embraces the values from both models and seeks a balance between the two.

With criminal law, as with ethics in general, there are often no clear-cut answers.

Because legal reasoning is all about comparing cases, the material in this book will be introduced the same way as it is in law school: through real-world cases showing issues in their full complexity.

PART ONE:

DECIDING WHAT BEHAVIOR TO CRIMINALIZE

People often use the word *crime* to mean "something bad"—but the legal definition of a crime is "an act that the law makes punishable." Nothing more, nothing less. If there is no law against a particular behavior, it isn't a crime, no matter how bad it is.

A crime is different from other forms of wrongdoing in that a crime is seen as harmful to society as a whole, which is why the police get involved and the government prosecutes and punishes people.

Human beings err, but not all bad behavior can be criminalized. In fact, criminalizing every bad or dangerous action would be impossible. Take smoking, for example. The National Center for Chronic Disease Prevention and Health Promotion calls smoking the single most preventable cause of disease and death in the United States. Smoking is harmful not just to the smoker, but to others through secondhand smoke. Smoking causes harm to all society by creating large medical costs, but smoking has a history in our culture of being socially acceptable, and not too long ago was even considered glamorous.

A society has to decide which wrong and harmful behaviors to criminalize. But how do we decide what to criminalize? How do we know if we are right?

CHAPTER 1

CRIMES OF OPPORTUNITY: THEFT — OR GOOD LUCK?

James Rogers walked into a bank with a check for $97.82 made out to his brother. He gave the check to the teller and, following his brother's instructions, asked her to deposit $80 into his brother's bank account and give him the remaining $17.82 in cash.

The teller wasn't sure how to do this, so she asked another employee how to handle the transaction. Her colleague told her she could deposit a check in part, and cash the remainder. The math was easy: just subtract the $80 from the original $97.82 and give James the change.

James signed the check, writing the date, December 6, 1959, as 12 06 59. The teller — according to the story that emerged later — confused the date of the check with the dollar amount and thought the amount was for $1,206.59. She deducted $80, which she deposited into the account, and put the change on the counter: $1,126.59.

One thousand dollars in 1959 was the equivalent of almost nine thousand today. James picked up the money and walked out of that bank with a windfall.

At the end of the day, the teller's cash box was short $1,108.77 — the amount the teller gave James minus the $17.82 she was supposed to have given him.

James was arrested, charged with bank robbery, and brought to trial.

According to traditional definitions, robbery requires taking something of value by force or threat, or by putting the victim in fear. The federal bank robbery statute under which James was convicted, however, defines bank robbery as "carrying away money belonging to a bank with the intent to keep the money." If the amount is over one thousand dollars, the crime is a felony, which is a serious crime. Carrying away less than one thousand dollars is also a crime, but a misdemeanor, which means a lighter punishment.

At his trial, James denied that the teller had given him the extra money. He said she gave him the $17.82 he was owed. The prosecutor submitted as evidence against James the tape from the teller's adding machine showing that she had accepted the check as having been written for $1,206.59.

The jury's task was to decide who was telling the truth.

Given the circumstances, there were two possible scenarios. The obvious explanation was that the teller made a mistake and James tried to profit from the mistake. The other possibility was that the teller pulled off a clever and elaborate hoax: She took the $1,108.77 for herself, and ran a tape to make it appear that she confused the date with the dollar amount so people would believe she had given James the money.

After listening to all the witnesses and weighing the evidence, the jury believed the bank teller.

The federal bank robbery law allows for imprisonment of up to ten years if the amount carried away is more than a thousand dollars.

James was convicted of bank robbery and sentenced to fifteen months in prison.

ANALYSIS OF THE JAMES ROGERS CASE

Law students and lawyers often use what is called IRAC (Issue, Rule, Analysis, Conclusion), a method of systematically applying the law to a set of facts. IRAC also provides a note-taking tool when legal analysis requires looking at lots of cases to understand the law, or trends in the law.

ISSUE: Was James Rogers guilty of felony bank robbery?

RULE: Bank robbery is defined as carrying away money belonging to a bank with the intent to keep the money. If the amount is over $1,000, the crime is a felony and carries harsher punishment than if the amount is under $1,000.

ANALYSIS: The "facts" in a case are whatever the jury believes. The facts in this case were these:

- James walked out of the bank with more than $1,000.
- The $1,000 belonged to the bank.
- James intended to keep the money. This can be inferred from the fact that he never tried to return the money.

The facts meet the requirements of the rule.

CONCLUSION: James was guilty of felony bank robbery.

• • • •

Should it be a crime to try to benefit from another person's mistake? After all, isn't that really what James Rogers did?

The phrase *bank robbery* suggests a masked bandit holding up a bank full of people at gunpoint and ordering the teller to hand over all the money. James did nothing like that. The teller handed him the money by mistake, and he walked out with it. It is unlikely he entered the bank intending to do anything wrong, and it is unlikely he tried to trick

CATEGORIES OF CRIMES

There are three broad categories of crimes: 1) crimes against the person, such as murder or battery, 2) crimes against property, such as theft or vandalism, and 3) vice or morality crimes, such as some forms of gambling and certain recreational drug use. Crimes that are *premeditated* are generally seen as more serious than crimes that are not. Examples of crimes that are not premeditated are crimes of opportunity and crimes springing from the heat of passion— for example, when a person suddenly behaves from impulse or overwhelming emotions.

the teller. This is what is called a crime of opportunity, which occurs when someone takes advantage of an unexpected situation.

Another situation in which people sometimes take advantage is finding something, knowing it belongs to someone else, and keeping it anyway. Take the case of Charles Newton and George Brooks.

Charles Newton traveled to Warren, Ohio, on October 24, 1878. He fastened his horse and buggy to a hitching post and went to attend some business. Later that afternoon, after he'd left Warren, he discovered that he had dropped a package with $200 in it ($200 then would be worth about $4,500 today).

Charles returned to Warren and searched everywhere he'd been. A team of horses was hitched to the place where he had fastened his horse, but he did his best to look for the package. He published notices of his loss in more than one newspaper, but he got no leads.

Almost a month later, a man named George Brooks was working with several other laborers on the street about five feet from the post where Charles had hitched his horse. He found the package buried in the mud, picked it up, and hid it in his pocket. Others were working nearby, but he didn't tell them what he had found. About half an hour after he found the money, the crew stopped for lunch. George quit work and asked to be paid.

He spent some of the money that very afternoon. A neighbor, seeing how much money he suddenly had, became suspicious and asked if he had stolen it. First he said he received the money from an uncle. Later he said, "What if I found it?"

He was arrested and charged with larceny, which simply means the theft of someone's personal property. At his trial, there was no evidence that he had seen any of the notices about the lost package. He was found guilty, though, because it was clear from his behavior that he knew the money belonged to someone else and he intended to keep it. Why else would he hide the money and not tell anyone he found it? Why else would he make no attempt to find the owner?

He appealed the decision but lost—which means that the majority of judges, or justices, in the court of appeals believed the trial court had reached the correct conclusion. One of the justices, however, disagreed with the decision. He thought that George had been less than honest, and that a person with higher morals would have tried to find the rightful owner. However, he did not believe that a scavenger who found something buried in the mud and kept it should be guilty of a crime.

APPEALS

A person who loses a trial can often appeal to a higher court. A higher court, or an appellate court, has the authority to overturn a lower court's decision if the decision was incorrect. Ordinarily, though, there is not a new trial, and new evidence cannot be introduced on appeal. The appellate court generally looks at the law applied by the trial court and makes sure that there was enough evidence to support the lower court's conclusion.

The law in Ohio remains the same today as it was in 1878: You can still be found guilty of larceny for finding something in the mud, hiding it, and not trying to find the owner.

The bank robbery statute under which James Rogers was convicted is still in effect as well. You can still be convicted of bank robbery for taking advantage of a teller's mistake.

•   •   •   •

Let's look at another example. Thirteen-year-old Brian Wrzesinski collected baseball cards. One day he was browsing in a store called Ball-Mart in a suburb of Chicago, Illinois. Ball-Mart specialized in baseball cards and other collectable items such as coins, autographed memorabilia, and Chicago sports items. In the shop, Brian spotted a 1968 card pairing the rookie stars Gerry Koosman and Nolan Ryan of the New York Mets. The card was in mint condition.

The price was listed—rather ambiguously—as "1200/."

Though he later admitted that he knew it was worth much more, Brian asked the sales clerk, "Is it worth twelve dollars?"

"Yes," the clerk said.

"I'll take it," he said.

Brian had twelve dollars in his pocket, so he bought the card.

More than twenty customers were in the shop at the time. The shop owner, Joe Irmin, was standing nearby, but later said he was busy waiting on other customers and didn't hear the exchange. The clerk who sold the card to Brian was not a regular store clerk. She was one of Joe's neighbors, helping out because the store had been unusually busy since Joe had started selling baseball cards.

Joe figured out that the clerk had sold the card for twelve dollars when other boys began coming into the store asking if Joe had any more of those twelve-dollar "Nolan Ryan specials."

The price, Joe explained later, had been $1,200, which he believed was the actual value of the card—not $12.00.

Joe posted a sign offering a hundred-dollar reward for information leading to the person who "stole" the card. Joe explained why he considered what Brian had done to be stealing: "He knew what he was doing and the girl didn't. He should have told her the card was worth more than twelve dollars. She didn't know if was worth twelve cents or twelve dollars or twelve hundred dollars. She just took the kid's word for it."

Brian viewed the situation differently. "I didn't steal the card or do anything wrong. I just went in there to see what they had. It was a card I was looking for. I knew the card was worth more than twelve dollars. I saw it priced for one hundred and fifty and up. I just offered twelve dollars for it and the lady sold it to me. People go into card shops and try to bargain all the time."

There was no law making it a crime to buy an item at less than the item's value, or less than the marked price. Joe, therefore, could not call the police and have Brian tracked down, arrested, and charged with theft or robbery. He was on his own.

After Joe learned who had the card—perhaps because

someone accepted his reward — he went to Brian's house and demanded the card back. Brian refused. The card, Brian said, was his. He had paid for it. He had the receipt.

Brian's father backed his son up. Shops like Ball-Mart, he reasoned, existed by taking advantage of starry-eyed kids who loved sports. Brian's father didn't think Joe had grounds for complaint if one of the kids who shopped in his store knew more about the value of cards than his clerk did. A Ball-Mart clerk had sold Brian the card for twelve dollars. A deal is a deal. End of story.

Because what Brian did wasn't a crime, Joe filed a civil lawsuit against Brian and asked the judge to make Brian return the card. Unlike crimes, which are charged by the government, civil lawsuits are simply disputes between citizens. With lawsuits, the court decides who is right and wrong and fashions a solution. In the case of Brian and the baseball card, the court would decide who should get the card.

CIVIL LAW VERSUS CRIMINAL LAW

Criminal law: Crimes are believed to endanger everyone, not just the individual victim. Crimes, therefore, are wrongdoings committed against the society as a whole. This is why a prosecutor on behalf of the government charges the crime. Criminal cases have names such as *People v. Jones* or *State v. Jones*. Those found guilty are punished.

Civil law: The dispute is between individual citizens. For example, if two people sign a contract and one breaches the contract, the other can sue in civil court. Other examples of civil disputes are injuries caused by noncriminal behavior. Anytime someone *sues* someone else, the matter is a civil dispute. With rare exceptions, there is no punishment in civil court. The court compensates victims by making sure they receive or are paid what they deserve, or resolves the dispute in some other way.

Joe's lawyer compared what Brian did to bank robbery. "If a bank sends you a check for two thousand dollars when it should have been twenty dollars," he explained in a press interview, "you can't pocket the two thousand on the grounds that the bank has to live with its mistake."

Before the court in Brian's case reached a decision, Brian and Joe came to an agreement. They decided to sell the baseball card and donate the proceeds to charity. On June 22, 1991, the card was auctioned by the Chicago Riverfront Antique Mart for $5,000.

• • • •

Newspapers and magazines ran stories about Brian and the baseball card. Many treated the incident lightly and with humor. The *Los Angeles Times* called the dispute "the greatest baseball story of the spring," and joked about whether a child with a superior knowledge of baseball cards and an understanding of decimal points poses a danger to society. A column published in the *Sporting News* called the dispute a "taffy pull" and offered a suggestion to Joe Irmin: Instead of suing Brian, hire him.

Other commentators were disturbed by the case. In the words of one:

> *[Brian] was wrong to take advantage of the store. There is no moral dilemma here, not even close. The father and son should stop posing proudly for TV and newspaper cameras and instead head over to the card store and hand back the Nolan Ryan rookie card.*

Another wondered:

What does it profit a boy to gain a coveted baseball card by a dubious means and learn nothing from the experience except to make sure he gets a receipt?

James Rogers committed a crime of opportunity when he knew the bank teller made a mistake but didn't tell her. George Brooks committed one when he knew someone lost the package of bank notes but made no attempt to find the owner.

What Brian did was arguably worse: He knew the card was worth more than he paid, and it appears he subtly tricked the clerk into selling it for only twelve dollars. He did not just simply take advantage of an unexpected opportunity; he cleverly manipulated the situation by the way he asked a question.

But whereas James and George were guilty of crimes, Brian was not.

The cases were heard in different courts in different states at different times, but these three cases suggest that it isn't always easy to decide which behavior should be criminalized. Moreover, the line between what to criminalize and what not to criminalize may not always be drawn in the right place.

CHAPTER 2

ANOTHER KIND OF BANK ROBBERY

One day in South St. Paul, Minnesota, a seventy-eight-year-old retired business owner named Walt Books was startled to open his bank statement and see that he had been charged $140 in fees. He could not understand why he had been charged so much money, so he went through his account records.

His bank records showed that he used his debit card to pay $3.09 for a cheeseburger and cup of coffee at McDonald's. That same day, he made a few other small purchases. When he made them, there was enough money in his account to cover the costs.

Later, however, when he made a larger purchase for $130, he had already withdrawn so much money that there was not enough in the account to cover the charge. The bank, therefore, refused to pay the $130. Like many banks, it also charged an amount called an overdraft fee as a penalty for trying to spend money he didn't have in his account. His bank charged $35 for each overdraft fee.

His overdraft fee should have been $35, not $140, because only one charge put him over the edge.

It turned out the bank's policy was to process the purchases out of order, putting the larger charge, for $130, first and the smallest one, for $3.09, last. As a result, the larger check drained his bank account. When the smaller charges were presented against his account, it was already empty, so the bank charged him three redundancy additional overdraft fees.

"They made one hundred and five dollars [extra] by doing nothing other than manipulating my account," Walt said. "It's crooked."

Another bank customer, Chuck Cano of Eden Prairie, Minnesota, was equally surprised to discover nine overdraft charges (more than $300 of them) on his bank account. Most were for small transactions that occurred before the charge that caused him to overdraw from his account.

"The bottom line is, it's a con job," said Chuck. He closed his account with Wells Fargo as a result of these charges.

Maxine Given, of Baltimore, Maryland, had a similar experience. She was charged a total of $370 in overdraft fees during April and May of 2009. She only overdrew twice, but because the banks reordered her transactions, she was charged multiple times.

Between the years of 2009 and 2011, lawsuits were filed against many of the country's major banks, including Bank of America, JP Morgan Chase, Union Bank, U.S. Bank, and Wachovia, accusing the banks of schemes like reordering debit charges so they could charge higher fees.

A lawsuit against National City Bank claimed that the bank provided false and misleading account balance information to customers, which led customers to believe they had more money in their accounts than they had, which in turn led the customers to overdraw on the accounts. When the customers, relying on the false information, tried to debit the money, the bank charged them an overdraft fee.

There were other procedures enabling banks to collect extra fees. For example, many banks had a policy of posting withdrawals ahead of deposits. This meant if a customer deposited $100 into an empty account in the morning, then later the same day withdrew $50, at the end of the day when the bank processed the transactions, the bank would process the $50 withdrawal first, charge the customer an overdraft fee, and then deposit the $100.

Not surprisingly, the customers who were charged the extra fees tended to be lower-income customers who were not able to maintain high balances in their accounts and whose accounts often went down closer to zero. This meant the victims of the banks' policies tended to be the customers least able to afford the extra charges.

The policy of reordering checks came about in the mid-1990s when the banks discovered that automatically reordering checks would dramatically increase their profits because they would be able to collect so much more money in overdraft fees. In 2002 U.S. banks collected approximately $6.2 billion in fees per year. Banks began increasing their charges for overdrafts, and by 2007, the amount collected was estimated at $50 billion.

Initially the banks defended themselves against the accusation that they were essentially fleecing their customers by saying that in reordering the charges, they had done nothing wrong. They said some customers appreciated the larger charge being processed first because those were usually the most important — mortgage payments, rent payments, car payments. In fact, the banks said some customers *wanted* the largest and most important charges processed first.

The defenders of the banks said that banks had the right to create any policies they chose, and if the customers didn't read the fine print carefully, well, *caveat emptor:* buyer beware.

The customers, in their lawsuits against the banks, accused the banks of intentionally reordering the transactions so the banks could collect hundreds of millions of dollars in extra fees.

One California judge declared the practice of reordering transactions high to low a way for banks to "gouge" their customers. The judge didn't believe customers would want a policy that could cause them to pay so much extra in fees. The banks continued to say they had done nothing wrong, but settled the cases by coming to an agreement outside of court.

Under the terms of the settlement, the banks agreed to pay back hundreds of millions of dollars to their customers. Because of the nature of a settlement—which is essentially a compromise so both sides can avoid lengthy and expensive trials—it is likely that the banks paid back only a portion of the unnecessary fees they collected. Some banks agreed, as part of their settlement, not to charge fees for overdraft charges under five dollars.

Though no criminal charges were ever filed against any bank executives who authorized these practices or any employees who carried them out, the nation's lawmakers drafted new laws and regulations preventing banks from overcharging customers in these ways.

You might say that banks overcharging customers to the tune of hundreds of millions of dollars gives a whole new meaning to the phrase *bank robbery,* providing an interesting contrast to James Rogers, who *was* convicted of robbing a bank when he took advantage of a teller's mistake.

CHAPTER 3

CHEATING? OR LUCKING INTO A GOOD DEAL?

On December 10, 1989, Timothy Childs was in John Ascuaga's Nugget Casino in Sparks, Nevada, playing a slot machine. He'd discovered that if he pulled the handle in a particular way, one of the three reels would stop spinning prematurely. As a result, he was able to manipulate the machine and win.

Karen Fleiner, an operations manager at the casino, was watching the gamblers through a special monitor, looking for irregular or suspicious behavior. After watching the way Timothy pulled the machine handle, she suspected him of cheating and called the Gaming Control Board. The Gaming Control Board sent an agent to the casino.

The agent, Robert Johnson, arrived at the casino within a few minutes of Karen Fleiner's call. As he watched, Timothy froze the reels several times.

Timothy was arrested, charged with cheating and burglary, and brought to trial. The case against Timothy seemed like a slam dunk, because a Nevada law specifically made it a crime to "vary the pull" of a slot machine handle. Because there was really no question that Timothy had varied the pull of the slot machine handle, the trial court found him guilty and, according to the penalty for violating that

TIMOTHY CHILDS AFTER ONE OF HIS ARRESTS FOR ALTERING
THE PULL OF THE HANDLE OF SLOT MACHINES.

particular statute, sentenced him to six years in the Nevada state prison.

Timothy appealed.

His case went to the Supreme Court of Nevada, which reversed the decision, finding that in fact Timothy was not guilty of cheating and burglary. The court said that because varying the pull doesn't damage the machine or alter the machine in any way, an innocent player not intending to cheat can very easily stumble across the technique and use it to his advantage. Some slot machine players move from one machine to another, hoping to increase their odds. Some players pull the handle very slowly or very quickly, hoping to increase their odds. If these things are not cheating — the court reasoned — how could varying the pull of the handle be cheating if the construction of the machine allowed for it without damaging the machine?

Furthermore, the court said that what Timothy had done — which came to be known as "handle popping" — was not like card crimping, in which a person alters the cards so he can increase his chances of winning. It wasn't like using mirrors, magnets, or other tools to increase the chance of winning. Handle popping, according to the court, was more like a player taking advantage of a dealer accidentally showing his cards.

• • • •

If courts are not supposed to create law, if they are only permitted to follow the law, how could the Nevada Supreme Court disregard the plain language of the statute that prohibited varying the pull and find Timothy not guilty?

Criminal laws, to be valid, must be *constitutional.* This means that laws must be in accord with requirements as given in the United States Constitution. To balance the powers, courts have the task of interpreting the Constitution and thus determining whether laws are constitutional.

The Constitution requires criminal laws to be clear and unambiguous, so that citizens are on notice that a particular behavior is considered criminal. The Nevada Supreme Court found Timothy not guilty by declaring the statute *constitutionally vague* and therefore not a valid law.

So what part of "it is prohibited to vary the pull of the handle" isn't clear?

The court reasoned that although varying the handle was prohibited, there were no specific instructions telling gamblers the proper way to pull the handle. Therefore, according to the court, the law was unconstitutionally vague and Timothy could not be convicted under it.

In its decision, the Nevada Supreme Court seemed to conclude that a gambler who didn't intend to cheat but simply took advantage of an opportunity in the form of a handle that could be manipulated should not be criminalized.

The day the Nevada Supreme Court reversed the trial

court's decision was a happy day for Timothy. Instead of spending six years in a Nevada prison, he walked away free.

• • • •

Proving himself to be a true gambler, Timothy Childs pushed his luck a little further. After the Nevada Supreme Court reversed his conviction, he went back to the casinos to pop some more handles. He probably figured, *Why not?* The Nevada Supreme Court had said it was legal.

He became good at finding slot machines with handles that could be popped. As before, he inflicted no damage on the machine. When casino officials again spied him pulling down on the handle and jerking it in such a way that the reels suddenly stopped spinning, enabling him to win easily, they called the police and had him arrested.

Again he was brought to trial. This time he was charged with "fraudulent slot machine manipulation." As before, the trial court found Timothy guilty. This time he was sentenced to ten years in prison.

As before, when his case went to the Nevada Supreme Court on appeal, a majority of the Supreme Court justices voted to overturn his conviction, reasoning that if the machine allowed for popping the handle without damaging the machine, they just couldn't see Timothy's behavior a crime deserving of imprisonment. One of the judges disagreed and felt it was clear that Timothy intended to cheat. The judge who wanted to convict Timothy was outvoted.

Once more, Timothy walked away free.

It was a crime for James Rogers to take advantage of a teller's mistake, but it was not a crime for Timothy Childs to take advantage of a handle that could be popped. Is there a good reason for the distinction? Or is it an arbitrary one?

Today most casinos have switched to digital slot machines without handles, thus solving what the casinos saw as a handle-popping problem, but not, of course, solving the larger problem of where to draw the line between cheating and winning fair and square.

• • • •

In 1804, a man named Mr. Woods — that really was his name — was selling lumber in a market in New York that specialized in a very expensive brand called braziletto wood. Mr. Woods was not the owner of the wood. He was acting as an agent, or salesperson. Mr. Woods sold some lumber to a Mr. Seixas. When Mr. Seixas bought the wood, Mr. Woods gave him a "bill of parcel" describing the item as braziletto wood. Mr. Seixas paid a high but fair price for the braziletto wood.

Later, Mr. Seixas discovered that Mr. Woods had in fact sold him inferior-quality wood known as peachum. He brought Mr. Woods to court and demanded his money back in exchange for the return of the wood.

The court applied the principle of *caveat emptor*. Buyer beware, as you might guess from the name, means it is the buyer's responsibility to make sure he knows exactly what he is buying. If the buyer makes a bad purchase, it is pretty much his or her tough luck.

When the case of Mr. Woods and Mr. Seixas came to court, the judge thought it was a clear case for Mr. Woods because Mr. Seixas had plenty of opportunity to examine the wood before he bought it. Mr. Woods gave no express written warranty, and—according to the court—the written description in the bill of parcels did not count as a written warranty.

Mr. Woods, according to the court, had done nothing wrong under the law and Mr. Seixas was not entitled to his money back.

Today, the case of Mr. Woods and Mr. Seixas might be decided differently because of consumer protection laws intended to shield consumers from being taken advantage of by sellers. In California and other states, for example, false advertising is a crime. A business or employee who lies about a product for sale in California can be sentenced to up to six months in jail.

In 1804 there were no such consumer protection laws in New York.

Laws change over time, evolving as the culture evolves. Behavior that one group of people living in a particular era choose to criminalize can seem acceptable to a different group of people, or people living in a different era. How, therefore, can any society be sure it is criminalizing behavior that is truly wrong?

CHAPTER 4

RACE: CHANGING ATTITUDES AND LAWS

In 1890, about twenty-five years after the Civil War ended and slaves were freed, Louisiana passed a law known as the Separate Car Act, making it illegal for a black person to ride in the same railroad car as white people. The law was called "an Act to promote the comfort of passengers." Under the law, any passenger not honoring the segregation could be fined up to twenty-five dollars, or given up to twenty days in jail.

Even in democracies in which lawmakers are elected by a majority, laws rarely represent the beliefs of all citizens. The Louisiana Separate Car Act was no exception. Immediately after the law was passed, a group of concerned citizens formed an organization called the Comité des Citoyen, or Committee of Citizens, dedicated to seeing the law repealed. Members of the group were both black and white.

Homer Plessy, a resident of the downtown Creole section of New Orleans and a shoemaker by trade, was destined to become the committee's most famous member.

Homer was born in New Orleans on St. Patrick's Day, 1863, a mere three months after Lincoln freed the slaves. During slave times, Homer's parents and grandparents had been members of a category of people in New Orleans known

HOMER PLESSY, WHO FOUGHT—UNSUCCESSFULLY AT THE TIME—TO CHANGE UNFAIR RACIAL DISCRIMINATION LAWS.

as "free people of color." Before the Civil War, free people of color were allowed to own property and keep their wages, but were nonetheless subjected to special laws. For example, free people of color were not allowed to insult a white person, or act as if they were equal to white people.

Homer was also what was then called an "octoroon," which meant that he was seven-eighths white. The fact that he was one-eighth black meant that under Louisiana law, he was considered "colored."

The Committee of Citizens cast around for a way to challenge the Separate Car Act. They could try to get the elected officials to repeal the law, which could succeed if a majority of citizens in the district were opposed to the law.

The committee didn't have much hope of convincing elected officials to change the Separate Car Act, because so many voters supported it. Their only recourse, therefore, was to challenge its constitutionality in court.

To challenge a law in court, however, someone has to first break the law and get arrested.

Some sources say Homer volunteered for the task. Others say the members of the committee persuaded Homer to get himself arrested. Whichever way it came about, Homer agreed to break the law to allow the committee to argue in court that it was unconstitutional. The committee planned to argue that segregation violated the rights of black people by denying them *equal protection* under the Fourteenth Amendment of the United States Constitution.

On June 7, 1892, Homer bought a ticket to ride Train Number Eight of the East Louisiana Railroad line. Ticket in hand, he crossed the terminal to the train, ignoring the "Colored Only" sign. He went directly to the first-class car and took a seat.

To make sure Homer was arrested, and to make sure he was arrested for violating the Separate Car Act instead of something else, the committee hired Christopher Cain, a private investigator and former Louisiana prison guard, to make the actual arrest. The committee also informed the railroad what they were doing, and asked for cooperation.

Shortly after the whistle blew and the train inched forward, the conductor, J. J. Dowling, passed through the car, collecting tickets. When he got to Homer, he asked, "Are you a colored man?"

"Yes," said Homer.

"Then you will have to retire to the colored car," said J. J. Dowling.

Homer replied that he was an American citizen who paid for his ticket and had the right to sit in the first-class car.

The conductor asked Homer again to leave. Again Homer refused. Other passengers stirred.

Dowling then signaled the engineer, who brought the train to a stop. Dowling got off the train and returned with Detective Cain, who told Homer to obey the law and go to the car designated for colored passengers.

Again Homer refused, saying he would rather go to jail than give up his seat.

Detective Cain forcibly pulled Homer from the train and arrested him. Train Number Eight resumed its trip to Covington.

• • • •

The judge, John Ferguson of the Criminal District Court for the Parish of New Orleans, rejected Homer's argument that segregation violated the Constitution. He found Homer guilty and fined him twenty-five dollars, but did not give him jail time.

The committee expected the judge to find Homer guilty. Any victory would have to happen on appeal, in a higher court. Homer appealed, and the United States Supreme Court agreed to hear his case.

In 1896, the United States handed down its opinion, entitled *Plessy v. Ferguson,* in which the Supreme Court upheld Homer's conviction and ruled that segregation did not violate the Constitution. The court reasoned that segregation

Supreme Court of the United States,

No. 210, October Term, 1895.

Homer Adolph Plessy
Plaintiff in Error,

vs.

J. H. Ferguson, Judge of Section "A"
Criminal District Court for the Parish
of Orleans.

In Error to the *Supreme* Court of the State of
Louisiana

This cause came on to be heard on the transcript of the record from the *Supreme* Court of the State of *Louisiana*, and was argued by counsel.

On consideration whereof, It is now here ordered and adjudged by this Court that the judgment of the said *Supreme* Court, in this cause, be, and the same is hereby, *Affirmed with costs.*

Per Mr. Justice Brown,
May 18, 1896.

Dissenting:
Mr. Justice Harlan

PLESSY V. FERGUSON SUPREME COURT DECISION.

did not imply that one race is inferior to the other—as long as the separate facilities were equal.

A PLAQUE ON HOMER PLESSY'S TOMBSTONE IN NEW ORLEANS, LOUISIANA.

The Supreme Court ruling in *Plessy v. Ferguson* ushered in what has been called the Jim Crow era, when laws were passed in many states requiring the races to be segregated, often making it a crime for people of different races to sit together, go to school together, or drink from the same drinking fountains. It was an era when black people were criminalized for doing what white people were allowed to do, an era of segregation and unfair race laws that lasted for decades.

• • • •

Early in the morning of December 7, 1941, a Japanese dive-bomber appeared through the clouds over Pearl Harbor, the American naval base on the Hawaiian island of Oahu. The bomber bore the symbol of the rising sun, a red circle fringed with bold rays against a white background. Behind the bomber came 360 Japanese warplanes, including torpedo bombers and other dive-bombers.

It was Sunday morning, so many of the American soldiers stationed at the base were attending church. Two radar

BOMBING OF PEARL HARBOR.

operators detected the aircraft approaching Pearl Harbor, but the operators were expecting a fleet of B-17s from the mainland, so they did not sound the alarm. Nobody was prepared for a military attack.

At 7:55 a.m. Hawaiian time, the Japanese attacked. Having achieved complete surprise, the Japanese destroyed much of the American aircraft fleet before the planes could get off the ground to fight back. The bombs fell for almost two hours. When the bombing was over, about 2,400 Americans were dead, and 21 ships and 188 planes had either been destroyed or damaged.

The attack was devastating. Americans were shocked, outraged, and frightened. The very next day, America declared war on Japan and entered World War II.

Newspapers carried anti-Japanese articles. One FBI agent, who was later fired for inventing a sensational rumor, declared that twenty thousand Japanese Americans were planning an armed uprising in San Francisco. Congressman John Rankin said, "I'm for catching every Japanese in America, Alaska, and Hawaii now and putting them in concentration camps." The secretary of war, Henry L. Stimson, said, "Their racial characteristics are such that we cannot understand or trust even the citizen Japanese."

Lieutenant General John L. DeWitt declared all Japanese and Japanese Americans dangerous. DeWitt told President Roosevelt that it was simply too difficult to tell which Japanese Americans were spies and which were not, so

JAPANESE AND JAPANESE AMERICANS WERE SENT TO INTERNMENT CAMPS.

all people of Japanese heritage had to be treated as potential spies.

President Roosevelt, in turn, signed an executive order giving the military the power to arrest and imprison without trial any people suspected of being a threat to national security, an order that paved the way for the internment of Japanese people living on the West Coast. Public Law 503, which was passed on March 1, 1942, made it a crime punishable by imprisonment or a fine for a person to ignore military evacuation orders.

• • • •

One young man, twenty-three-year-old Fred Korematsu, didn't believe he should have to give up his freedom. He was an American citizen, born in Oakland, California. His parents, Japanese immigrants, earned their living by operating a flower nursery. He grew up speaking English as his native language and living the life of an ordinary American boy.

He'd always been a loyal American. In fact, after high school Fred tried to join the United States Coast Guard because he wanted to fight for his country, but the recruiter didn't allow him to fill out the application because of his race.

So when the evacuation orders came, Fred made false identification papers stating that his name was Clyde Sarah, and that he was a Spanish Hawaiian born in Las Vegas. He changed his name on his draft card and he and his girlfriend, Ida, who was Italian American, made plans to run away to Nevada and get married there. When the time came to leave, though, she had second thoughts about leaving her family. To be near her, Fred remained in California, passing himself off as non-Japanese.

Then one Saturday afternoon, he was waiting for Ida in nearby San Leandro when he ducked into a drugstore to make a small purchase. Someone in the drugstore must have recognized him, because a few minutes later, when he and

FRED KOREMATSU AS A YOUNG MAN.

Ida were walking down the street, two police officers stopped him, handcuffed him, and took him to the San Leandro Jail.

Fred was convicted in federal court of violating Public Law 503. Because the judge was impressed with Fred's testimony about his loyalty to America and his desire to fight for his country, he sentenced him to a five-year probationary period instead of a prison sentence.

He wasn't allowed to go free, though. As soon as the judge said he would not be sentenced to federal prison, he was promptly arrested by military officials and taken to a Japanese detention center in central Utah, where he spent the entire war. Unlike the others in the detention camp, he had an actual criminal conviction. He was therefore shunned by many of the frightened inmates, who saw him as a troublemaker.

He appealed his conviction all the way to the United States Supreme Court. The Supreme Court ruled that his arrest and conviction were legal because the government is justified in forced evacuations during times of national emergency and peril.

After the war, Fred—branded a criminal—never stopped believing that he was innocent and never gave up trying to get his conviction overturned. In 1980, President Carter appointed a special commission to look into the imprisonment of Japanese Americans during World War II. The commission concluded that there was never any evidence that people of Japanese descent on the West Coast posed any danger.

In 1988, Congress apologized and granted compensation of $20,000 to each surviving detainee to help compensate them for the loss of their homes and property, and for the humiliation and hardship endured.

The U.S. District Court in San Francisco reversed Fred's conviction on November 10, 1984. He stood in the court that day and said, "I would like to see the government admit they were wrong and do something about it so this will never happen to any American citizen of any race, creed, or color."

• • • •

On Tuesday, September 11, 2001 — for the first time since Pearl Harbor — foreign enemies launched a devastating attack against Americans on American soil.

Terrorists hijacked four American passenger planes and flew two of the planes into the north and south towers of the World Trade Center complex in New York City. Both towers collapsed within two hours. The hijackers flew a third plane into the Pentagon in Washington, D.C. The fourth

The Pentagon after the attack of hijacked American Airlines Flight 77 the morning of September 11, 2001.

plane crashed in Pennsylvania after the passengers attempted to take control from the hijackers. Almost three thousand people died in the attacks.

As in 1945 after the bombing of Pearl Harbor, Americans were shocked, outraged, and frightened.

Osama bin Laden, leader of al-Qaeda, a militant group of Muslims in the Middle East, took credit for the attacks.

This time, the face of the attacker was Middle Eastern and Muslim.

• • • •

Shortly before the attack on September 11, 2001, Huzaifa Parhat and sixteen of his countrymen left China and resettled in the Tora Bora mountains of Afghanistan. Huzaifa and the group of men he traveled with were members of the Uyghur (pronounced "WEE-gur") people, an ethnic minority originally from an area in what is now Turkey. Uyghur people live in China, Afghanistan, Pakistan, and Turkey. Most Uyghurs are Muslim.

Huzaifa and his companions left China because the Uyghur people have long been discriminated against there, and because they did not agree with the actions of the Chinese communist government. When they arrived in the Tora Bora mountains, they lived in a camp run by a Ugyhur group called the Eastern Turkistan Islamic Movement.

After the attack of September 11, the American military bombed Afghanistan, particularly the Tora Bora mountains, where the Americans believed Osama bin Laden and other al-Qaeda members were hiding.

The bombing destroyed the camp in which Huzaifa and his companions were living, so they fled to nearby Pakistan.

HUZAIFA PARHAT (ALSO KNOWN AS ABLIKIN TURAHUN).

They were captured by Pakistanis and turned over to the American military as "enemy combatants" in exchange for a great deal of money—so much money, in fact, that a court later described the transaction as a sale.

At about this time, the United States military set up a detention center in Guantanamo Bay, Cuba, for imprisoning suspected terrorists. The United States military claimed that the laws of war allowed them to hold enemy combatants for the duration of the war and try them by a military tribunal, a special kind of court set up to try enemies during wartime. Instead of regular juries, military officers decide whether the accused is guilty.

President George W. Bush's administration used military tribunals to put people on trial who had been captured abroad and held at a prison camp at Guantanamo Bay.

Huzaifa was one of those individuals. The tribunal found that he and his companions had been armed because they intended to fight against the Chinese government, not the United States. However, there remained an accusation that the Uyghur independence group to which Huzaifa and the others belonged was associated with al-Qaeda; therefore, they themselves were associated with al-Qaeda and were enemies. But nobody explained in what way the Uyghur independence group was associated with al-Qaeda. There was no evidence that Huzaifa or any of his companions ever fought against America or even intended to, but the military tribunal concluded that because Huzaifa was associated with the Uyghur independence group, which was associated with al-Qaeda, Huzaifa was an enemy combatant.

He was sentenced to prison for the duration of the war.

In 2005, Congress passed the Detainee Treatment Act, which allowed enemy combatants imprisoned in Guantanamo Bay to appeal their convictions. Huzaifa immediately filed an appeal.

His appeal came to court in 2008—after Huzaifa had been in prison for seven years. The United States District Court declared the conviction of Huzaifa not valid. Guilt by distant association was not enough.

The American military, however, refused to release him. The military conceded that they did not have enough evidence—under the usual standards of reliability—to imprison Huzaifa and his companions. However, the armed forces said regular courts should not interfere and that the military courts should have the power to decide who is designated an enemy combatant in times of war. Also, the military stated that Cuba was not a United States territory, so what the armed forces did in Cuba was not subject to United States law. It is worth noting that this wasn't a military decision alone — the president and Congress could have stopped it, but didn't.

In 2011, after a few more rounds of appeals and delays — and after Huzaifa had spent more than a decade in prison — he was finally released in El Salvador.

• • • •

When the detention camp at Guantanamo Bay was first established and it appeared that Muslims were being targeted, Fred Korematsu spoke out, urging the American government not to make the same mistakes in targeting Muslims that had been made in targeting Japanese people during World War II. In fact, he filed what is known as an amicus brief in April 2004 in response to the arrests of Muslims. He wrote, "Full vindication for the Japanese Americans will arrive only when we learn that, even in times of crisis, we must guard against prejudice and keep uppermost our commitment to law and justice."

After a lifetime of activism against the criminalization of people based on race and prejudice, Fred Korematsu died in 2005 — while Huzaifa was still imprisoned in Guantanamo Bay.

As cultural attitudes change, the nation's laws also change. After the attack on Pearl Harbor, many people genuinely believed Fred was dangerous and should be imprisoned. Looking back, it's easy to see the error. It's harder, though, for people to see their own mistakes at the time the mistakes are being made.

CHAPTER 5

DECIDING WHAT IS A DANGER TO SOCIETY

In 1868, in Wilkes County, North Carolina, Elizabeth Rhodes accused her husband of beating her. She brought charges against him for assault and battery.

Elizabeth's husband, A. B. Rhodes, freely admitted to beating his wife, but defended himself by explaining that she had said something to him that he hadn't liked. The problem was, he couldn't remember exactly what she had said.

The evidence presented at his trial showed that he struck her three times with a switch about the size of one of his fingers but not as large as his thumb. The size of the switch was important because under common law as understood by this particular court, a man could legally beat his wife if the switch he used was no bigger than his thumb—the so-called rule of thumb.

• • • •

Courts are not supposed to make law. They are supposed to apply

> **COMMON LAW AND THE RULE OF THUMB**
>
> Statutes are laws that are written and passed by elected officials in a legislature. Common law, in contrast, comes from custom and usage. Common law originated in England and later passed to many of the U.S. states. In some states, even today, common laws are considered so basic that they are often applied without reference to any written laws. The "rule of thumb" was derived from common law.

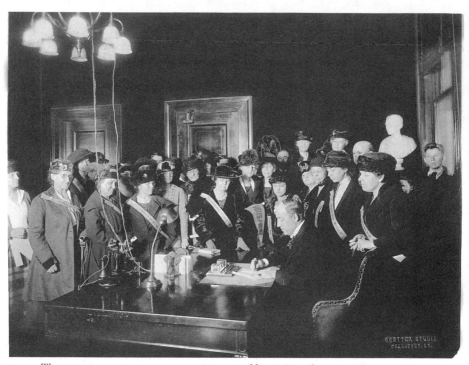

and follow statutes. But written statutes often do not cover all possibilities that might occur in real life, so when interpreting the law, courts occasionally create rules and carve out exceptions to statutes. If the legislature doesn't like the way courts are interpreting statutes or deciding cases, the legislature can pass new laws or clarify the existing laws.

Since whatever Elizabeth said to irritate her husband had left so little impression that he was not even able to recall it, the trial court concluded that she had done nothing to deserve the beating. Nonetheless, the court found Elizabeth's husband not guilty of assault and battery because the switch he used was smaller than his thumb.

Elizabeth's case went on appeal to the North Carolina

Supreme Court. The argument made on her behalf there, as in the trial court, was that assault and battery was a crime. Her husband had assaulted and battered her. Therefore, he was guilty of a crime.

The North Carolina Supreme Court agreed with the trial court's decision that Elizabeth's husband was not guilty, but gave a different reason. When courts of appeal make their decisions, also called opinions, they often go to great lengths to explain the reason for their decision. This makes it easier for other courts to follow their ruling, and lets people know how the court will respond to certain behavior.

The court began its explanation by pointing out that North Carolina law does not recognize the right of the husband to beat his wife. In fact, the violence inflicted on Elizabeth would certainly be considered battery—if Elizabeth had not been the man's wife. However, the court felt that finding Elizabeth's husband guilty would cause a greater danger to society than whatever harm she sustained from his battering her.

The court, however, did not like the rule of thumb. What mattered—according to this court—was not the size of the switch but how severe the injuries were. The court framed the issue in this way: "The question is therefore plainly presented, whether the court will allow conviction of the husband for moderate correction of the wife without provocation."

As soon as a court describes a husband beating his wife as giving her "moderate correction," it's pretty clear the court doesn't frown on the behavior. Indeed, after giving its conclusion that "family government" is "complete in itself," the court said: "We will not interfere with or attempt to control [families] in favor of either husband or wife, unless in cases where permanent or malicious injury is inflicted or threatened, or the condition of the party is intolerable."

The court explained that interfering in marital disputes would cause more harm than good because a wife could—and should—forget "temporary pain," but if she took her domestic quarrel public, the pain of public humiliation for the family would not be easily forgotten and would cause more long-term damage to the family. Moreover, the court reasoned, courts should not try to resolve domestic quarrels because there was no way to really know who was at fault. After all, "Who can tell what significance the trifling words may have had to the husband? Who can tell what happened an hour before, and every hour for a week?"

The court went on to explain that the differences between the lower and upper classes also made it too difficult to delve into private family matters:

> *Suppose a case came to us from a hovel, where neither delicacy of sentiment nor refinement of manners is appreciated or known. The parties themselves would be amazed, if they were to be held responsible for rudeness or trifling violence. What do they care for insults and indignities? In such cases what end would be gained by investigation or punishment?*

How, the court concluded, could the same law possibly apply to the upper and lower economic classes?

Bring all these cases into court side by side, with the same offense charged and the same proof made, and what conceivable charge of the court to the jury would be appropriate to all the cases, except that they all have domestic government, which they have formed for themselves, suited to their own peculiar conditions, and that these governments are supreme.

What all this meant, for the North Carolina Supreme Court in 1886, was that "every household [had] and must have a government of its own, modeled to suit the temper, disposition, and condition of its inmates," and courts meddling in family matters threatened the freedom and autonomy of families, and hence posed a greater danger to society than a husband assaulting his wife.

• • • •

The North Carolina Supreme Court's attitude toward women in 1886 was common in that era. Women in the nineteenth century were not allowed to vote. They rarely had a formal education or a well-paid job, so they were almost always financially dependent on their husband. The state of Illinois, for example, refused to let women become lawyers. One justice of the Illinois Supreme Court, in explaining why he agreed with the decision, explained that family organization is founded on "divine laws" as well as the "nature of things," which decreed that certain functions belonged to womanhood and certain functions did not. According to Illinois law, a woman's role was to take care of children and home.

For almost one hundred years after Elizabeth's case, wives' complaints that their husbands battered them were largely ignored by police and courts. Things began to change in the 1960s and 1970s.

Between 1975 and 1980, forty-five states passed laws protecting women from violence in the home. In 1994, the United States Congress passed the Violence Against Women's Act (VAWA), recognizing that, at least in the eyes of the federal government if not all of the states, domestic violence is a crime. Between 1997 and 2003, more than seven hundred new domestic violence–related laws were created.

Although not all states specifically name domestic violence as a crime—and not all states take it equally seriously—no states today recognize "spousal exceptions" to the laws against assault and battery. And, naturally, the rule of thumb is no longer good law anywhere in the United States.

Thus, whereas the nineteenth-century North Carolina Supreme Court believed that courts meddling in private family affairs presented a greater danger to society than domestic violence did, today the more common view is that spousal abuse constitutes a greater danger to society.

What people see as dangerous varies, evolving and changing as cultural attitudes and fears change. A crime, remember, is different from other forms of wrongdoing in that a crime is seen as harmful to society as a whole, which is why the police get involved and the government prosecutes and punishes people. Which behavior is criminalized, therefore, is often linked to evolving cultural attitudes.

All of this raises a question: Are there, in fact, behaviors that are always wrong, no matter what?

CHAPTER 6

KILLING IS A CRIME, EXCEPT WHEN IT ISN'T

What about killing? Isn't it always wrong to kill people?

Perhaps we should take a look at the laws governing murder and how they are applied.

In the Pakistani city of Abbattabad — a city known for its pleasant weather, premier schools, and military establishment — a three-story concrete compound lay at the end of a dirt road. The concrete walls were topped with barbed wires, as were most of the houses in that area.

Many aspects of the compound, though, were a little odd. This compound seemed just a little too large for the area. The wall around the perimeter was twelve feet high with a walled-in balcony. There were no telephone wires leading to the house. Whoever lived inside burned their trash instead of sending it out. The house had no air conditioning, despite its location in a luxurious neighborhood with softly lit backyards, well-manicured landscaping, and swimming pools.

The American Central Intelligence Agency, the CIA, watched the compound through satellites to try to figure out who was living there. CIA agents rented a home in Abbattabad, from which a team observed the compound over a number of months. They concluded the compound had been built to hide someone. Immediately they suspected that the person hiding was Osama bin Laden, the man behind the attacks of September 11, 2001. After months observing the building, one of the CIA agents, going at least partly on intuition, became convinced that Osama bin Laden lived there, but nobody was ever able to photograph him in the compound. The CIA agents believed he was living there with at least one of his wives, most likely the youngest, and a few of his children.

On May 2, 2011, twenty-four members of the United States Naval Special Warfare Development Group (DEVGRU) — also formerly known as SEAL Team Six — set out on a secret mission, approved by President Barack Obama.

They entered the compound and found — and ultimately killed — Osama bin Laden.

• • • •

The killing of Osama bin Laden and four other residents of the compound — while generally well received by Americans and the American news media — sparked an international controversy. International opinion was generally divided into two groups: those who felt the United States had been fully justified in targeting and shooting bin Laden, and those who felt that what the U.S. government had done was against the law.

International law makes it illegal to assassinate a political leader, but legal to kill an enemy combatant. So whether the killing of bin Laden was legal under international law depends on whether he was a political leader or an enemy combatant.

To complicate matters, it is against the law to kill an

enemy combatant if he tries to surrender. In fact, under international law, enemy combatants should be given the opportunity to surrender.

Those who felt the killing of Osama bin Laden was illegal pointed out that the military played the role of judge, jury, and executioner. The SEALs, according to this argument, should have tried to capture him and bring him to trial. Others respond that this would have been too dangerous, and others residents in the house may have died had the SEALs not killed him as quickly as possible.

A further complication is that it isn't clear what the orders actually were, because official reports were vague, and the SEALs who participated gave different accounts of what they understood the orders to be.

•　•　•　•

Case law, or court-created common law, is about drawing rules from cases. If killing Osama bin Laden was legal, this might be the rule:

> *A soldier in a national army who kills while acting under orders from the president or other head of state is not guilty of a crime.*

One problem with this rule is that it doesn't include war crimes—for example, the behavior of the Nazis in Germany during World War II who, as members of a national army acting under the orders of a head of state, killed millions of innocent civilians. Claiming that one was "acting under orders" has not generally been a successful defense for committing an atrocity.

The real problem is that once you say "Killing in that particular instance was okay," you take your first step on what might be called a slippery slope—when taking one small step leads to another and another, and you end up where you don't want to be. Once you say "Killing is not a crime in this instance," you have to decide where to draw the line.

On one end of the spectrum, there are killings that are obviously heinous crimes and completely unjustified—such as an armed person opening fire on a school and murdering children. On the other end, there are killings that, strictly speaking, may violate international laws of war, such as the assassination of Osama bin Laden and others in the compound, but that many in the United States believe should not be considered a crime.

Where do we draw the line between these two extremes? It's much easier to be consistent when taking an extreme position such as "Killing is always a crime. There are no exceptions." But if you say "Killing is always a crime," you have to label the killing of Osama bin Laden a crime, which means arresting the SEALs for murder.

So how about this rule:

There are exceptions to the rule that killing is a crime, but we have to look at each case individually to decide whether it should be considered an exception.

However, many killers who are brought to trial can probably give at least some justification for why they killed their victim—so we're right back to where we started, with no working rule. Additionally, with a vague case-by-case rule, nobody would know ahead of time what they could or couldn't do. From the phrasing of the rule, people might get the idea that they could get away with killing someone if they felt it was justified.

Whereas rules that are too general are too difficult to apply, rules that are too specific are also problematic because the rule may include instances that the writers of the law didn't foresee.

• • • •

War is one common context in which killings are usually not crimes. "Collateral damage," the killing of innocent civilians, is often accepted as a tragic but unavoidable consequence of war. "Targeted killing," which many claim is illegal, is a government's targeting a particular person, considered an enemy, and sending the military to carry out the killing. The targeted killing of Osama bin Laden was only one instance of many targeted killings by Americans. In fact, the SEAL who killed Osama bin Laden told an interviewer that SEALs went on such missions into private residences "every night." Often, as in the raid of Osama bin Laden's compound, others living in the home are also killed, and sometimes children are caught in the crossfire.

In the words of Rory Little, a criminal law professor and former federal prosecutor, "Some killers are put in the electric chair, others are given medals of honor."

• • • •

Anthony Fowlin was in a crowded nightclub in Easton, Pennsylvania, in the early-morning hours of December 12, 1993. At least two hundred people were in the nightclub.

51

Three men approached Anthony. One pepper-sprayed his eyes. Another drew a gun.

Anthony too was armed. Later he explained that he knew these men and feared for his life, so he drew his own handgun and, unable to aim accurately with pepper spray in his eyes, fired more than seven times in the general direction of the attackers.

He killed one of the attackers and injured another. He also shot and wounded Valerie Lewis, an innocent bystander who was at least fifteen feet away.

Immediately after the shooting, Anthony left the nightclub and surrendered to the Easton police.

Initially Anthony was charged with various crimes, including murder, but before the case came to trial, the prosecutor dropped the majority of charges on the grounds of justifiable self-defense, meaning Anthony was adequately provoked, the force he used to defend himself was not excessive given the situation, and he couldn't reasonably have been expected to retreat under the circumstances.

Anthony was brought to trial, though, to determine if he was guilty of the remaining charge of recklessly endangering innocent bystanders when he fired repeatedly in the general direction of the attackers. After all, the nightclub was crowded. He had pepper spray in his eyes, so he should have known he couldn't aim well.

The judge in the trial court had difficulty figuring out which law to apply. In some other states, if a person acts in self-defense, he is not criminally liable for the injury or death of innocent bystanders. But there were no statutes or cases to turn to for precedent in Pennsylvania.

The trial court believed a person acting in justifiable self-defense could still be found guilty of murdering or injuring innocent bystanders if he behaved recklessly, but before Anthony was put on trial, the judge in the case asked the Pennsylvania Supreme Court which law to apply.

The Pennsylvania Supreme Court applied a doctrine called transferred intent, which says that if while acting in self-defense someone injures or kills an innocent bystander but didn't *intend* to kill or injure him or her, that person has not commited a crime. The doctrine of transferred intent is not the law in all states.

Thus, Anthony's right to shoot his attackers in self-defense was transferred to a right to shoot in a way that endangered innocent bystanders, as long as his intent was simply to defend himself. Under the doctrine of transferred intent as applied in Pennsylvania, the shooting would not have been a crime even if Anthony had killed Valerie Lewis.

• • • •

Sometimes killings are carried out by governments instead of individuals. One example is the death penalty, sanctioned in many states. Those who favor the death penalty argue that people who commit certain violent crimes such as murder or torture deserve to die, and that maintaining social order requires that criminals get what they deserve. Other proponents of the death penalty believe that it will discourage people from committing murder if they know it will cost them their own life.

But capital punishment inevitably raises the question: What if the state makes a mistake and kills an innocent person?

Timothy Baldwin was accused of beating and murdering his elderly neighbor, a family friend, on the evening of April 4, 1978. Timothy, who was thirty-eight at the time, had no history of violence. He insisted he was innocent, and said he had been traveling and spent the evening and night of the killing at a motel seventy miles from the crime scene.

There was no forensic evidence connecting him to the murder. There was, however, evidence that Timothy's van had been parked in front of the house that night. Witnesses said they saw a scuffle of some kind inside the house while the van was parked in front, but they thought it was a domestic quarrel. There were no fingerprints or any other solid evidence linking Timothy to the murder.

He was sentenced to be executed in Louisiana's electric chair.

Ten days before his execution, he filed special appeals on the grounds that he had been able to locate a receipt showing that he had indeed checked in to the motel seventy miles away, so he could not have committed the murder.

He asked for a new hearing so the new evidence could be examined. He said if given a new trial, he could prove he had checked in to the motel within an hour of the killing.

His appeal was denied on the grounds that even with the receipt, it was still possible he was guilty because the receipt merely showed that he checked in to the White Sands Motel seventy miles away in Arkansas. This *suggested* he was innocent but didn't prove his innocence. The court said it would not grant another trial simply because the receipt showed he *might* be innocent. The new evidence had to be stronger.

Timothy maintained that he was innocent until his last moments. His final statement was to congratulate everyone who had "tried so hard" to murder him: "I definitely have to give them credit as it takes a very special kind of person to murder an innocent man and be able to live with themselves."

He died in Louisiana's electric chair on September 10, 1984.

The killing was legal, but very possibly morally wrong.

The Center for Wrongful Convictions at the Northwestern University School of Law has compiled a list of people who have been executed even though they were most likely innocent of the crime for which they died. Timothy's name is one of many on their list.

•　•　•　•

There are numerous instances in which killing is not a crime. Deciding when a killing should be criminalized and punished isn't always an easy task—it's frequently a matter of opinion, depending on cultural views and norms. If what is morally wrong is not always punished, and what is punished is not always wrong—even in instances of killing—can we be sure we are criminalizing only the people who are genuinely bad and deserve punishment?

PART TWO:

PUNISHMENT

If choosing what to criminalize is difficult and filled with moral pitfalls, punishment—particularly government-imposed punishment—is even more problematic.

James Rogers was sentenced to fifteen months in prison for walking out of the bank with the extra money the teller handed him by mistake. Fifteen months in prison might not sound like that long when you consider that many sentences are fifteen, twenty, thirty years—or more. But think about fifteen months. Prisoners are locked up, dressed in prisoner garb, and watched constantly. Four hundred and fifty-five days living under oppressive and humiliating conditions.

"Going to prison is like dying with your eyes open," said Bernard Kerick, a disgraced New York Police commissioner who pleaded guilty to fraud and was sentenced to four years in prison. The horrors of life behind bars have been documented by countless memoirs, and confirmed by guards: Inmates are attacked, often by one another, sometimes by guards. They are occasionally given lengthy periods of solitary confinement. Imprisonment is hard on the convicted person's family and children, as well, often leading to the breakup of families. The California Research Bureau has pointed out that imprisonment harms the children of inmates:

Children whose parents have been arrested and incarcerated . . . have experienced the trauma of sudden separation from their sole caregiver. . . . The behavioral consequences can be severe, absent positive intervention — emotional withdrawal, failure in school, delinquency and risk of intergenerational incarceration.

• • • •

Of course, a prison sentence is not supposed to be a picnic. It's supposed to hurt the person who committed the crime. Punishment is, after all, defined as the deliberate infliction of pain or loss for an offense, sin, or fault.

Today in the United States, almost seven million people are imprisoned or serving some form of supervised sentence such as parole or probation. That's one out of every thirty-four adult Americans. Other countries imprison a far lower percentage of people. America's percentage of citizen imprisonment is five times higher than Great Britain's, nine times higher than Germany's and Libya's, and thirteen times higher than Japan's.

• • • •

Sometimes punishment is permanent—as with the death sentence. Sometimes it lasts only a few days.

Given the far-reaching pain of government-inflicted

PRISON POPULATIONS

This chart was compiled by the International Centre for Prison Studies, an organization that partners with the University of Essex. The number given is the prison rate per 100,000 people of the national population. The countries at the top of the chart imprison the largest percentage of their population.

COUNTRY	RATE OF IMPRISONMENT PER 100,000 PEOPLE	PERCENTAGE OF POPULATION IN PRISON
United States of America	716	0.716%
Cuba	510	0.510%
Rwanda	492	0.492%
Russian Federation	481	0.481%
El Salvador	422	0.422%
Iran	284	0.284%
Brazil	274	0.274%
Chile	270	0.270%
Saudi Arabia	162	0.162%
United Kingdom & Wales	148	0.148%
France	102	0.102%
Switzerland	82	0.082%
Libya	81	0.081%
Germany	80	0.080%
Syria	58	0.058%
Japan	54	0.054%

The figures for the United States correspond with the statistics given by the United States Department of Justice, which reports that 2,239,751 people were incarcerated in U.S. prisons and jails in 2011. The U.S. population is approximately 314 million. The math works out to just over 700 people imprisoned per 100,000.

punishment, the damage done to communities when lots of members are imprisoned, and the problems that arise when punishment is carried out by a bureaucracy, it is worth asking *why* we punish those who commit crimes.

CHAPTER 7

RETRIBUTION — "AN EYE FOR AN EYE"

Retribution—the idea that punishment is about giving people what they deserve—has roots deep in ancient Middle Eastern civilization. A Mesopotamian king named Hammurabi wrote a criminal code embodying the theory of retribution. He wanted written laws for consistency throughout his realm, and he wanted to make sure people who committed crimes got what—in his opinion—they deserved.

A number of punishments from Hammurabi's code probably strike the modern reader as either too harsh or not harsh enough. To take a few examples:

- If a son strikes his father, his hand shall be cut off.
- If a man hits a woman so that she loses her unborn child, he shall pay ten shekels for her loss.
- If anyone is caught committing robbery, he shall be put to death.
- If a man makes an accusation against a man and cannot prove it, the accuser shall be put to death.

By today's standards, a small fine for battering a woman and causing her to miscarry seems like too light a punishment for such violence. On the other hand, cutting off the hand

of a son who strikes his father seems too harsh. Wouldn't a literal eye for an eye simply require the father to hit the son back? But in a culture that finds it acceptable for a father to strike his child—as many cultures did until fairly recently and some still do—the father hitting the son back would not restore the balance of justice. While sons were forbidden to strike their fathers, fathers were expected to discipline their sons by whipping them.

Punishment that fits the crime under this view is not cruel because it is *deserved*.

The nineteenth-century German philosopher Immanuel Kant was famous for his strict views of retribution. He believed that a person guilty of a crime should get back exactly what he gave out. Under Kant's theory, failing to punish all wrongdoings creates an imbalance in the universe that endangers everyone's well-being: If people don't get what they deserve, the entire society loses its moral balance.

Punishment that fits the crime under Kant's theory is not cruel because it *serves a higher good.*

Many of the problems in any criminal justice system, including the basic problem of deciding what behavior to punish, undermine the theory that people who are punished get what they deserve. As we saw in Part I, what is morally wrong or dangerous is not always criminalized, and what is criminalized is not always dangerous or morally wrong. Retribution assumes that people get the punishment they deserve when they break a law, but if crimes are culturally determined, punishment does not necessarily fall on people who are bad. Smokers, remember, are not punished even though what they do is potentially dangerous to themselves and others. But Fred Korematsu was punished, and he posed no danger and did nothing wrong.

Another problem is determining what constitutes just deserts. The ancient expression of retribution "an eye for an eye" means you get back exactly what you give out. But people in jail are getting back something different from what they gave out. A person who steals is put in jail. An eye for an eye would require that, literally, someone would steal from *him*. So a problem with retribution is deciding how much jail time or other punishment is the correct measure. How much time should someone spend in jail for petty theft? A few days? A few weeks? How about kidnapping? A few years? A lifetime? Any measure of punishment must be, to some extent, arbitrary and a matter of opinion.

Another problem is that not all crimes are reported, and not all reported crimes result in a person getting caught and brought to court. Retribution assumes that the people who are punished deserve it, and the people who are not punished deserve not to be. But because most crimes never result in an arrest or punishment, retribution falls only on the minority who get caught.

Sometimes the likelihood of a person getting caught has nothing to do with the crime itself. For example, suppose one person lives in a large house with a big yard and a tall fence, with the nearest neighbors a half mile away. Another person lives in a crowded city apartment with thin walls, and neighbors can hear everything that happens. If both commit a crime in their home, the person in the crowded city apartment is more likely to get caught because neighbors are likely to see or hear something.

To take another example, people who are cleverer, or better liars, are less likely to get caught. One court-accepted way to measure human intelligence is with a score called an intelligence quotient, or IQ, which is derived through a test and formula. The test is standardized, and the results are factored with a person's age. IQ is generally categorized like this:

145 and over = genius
130–144 = gifted
115–129 = above average
85–114 = average
70–84 = below average
55–69 = challenged
40–54 = severely challenged

Early in the twentieth century, people with extremely low IQ were often believed to be threatening or dangerous. By the middle of the twentieth century, however, scientists and psychologists put forward convincing evidence that people with low intelligence were not more likely to commit crimes than other people.

It is generally accepted today among psychologists and scientists that low IQ rarely causes people to commit crimes.

However, statistics show that people with a low IQ are more likely to be arrested, charged, and convicted than people with a higher IQ. Less than 2 percent of the population has an IQ below 70, but between 12 and 20 percent of current death row inmates have an IQ below 70.

If a low IQ does not cause a person to commit crimes, why are so many more people with a low IQ facing the death penalty?

One answer offered by researchers is that people with lower intelligence are less able to withstand the pressure of being questioned by the police. It is easier to lead — or confuse — individuals with an unusually low intelligence, so they are more likely to incriminate themselves, or say something incriminating even if they are not guilty.

In addition, people with a low IQ often have an incomplete or immature idea of cause and blame, so under the pressure of police interrogation or cross-examination are more likely to confess to a crime they did not commit, or say things on the witness stand that may give the appearance of guilt. People with a low IQ may not be able to assist as well with their own defense or may not be aware of the intricacies of certain laws.

Retribution that falls more heavily on people who are in this position cannot restore balance fairly.

• • • •

Marvin Wilson, a resident of Texas charged with capital murder, had an IQ of 61 if you believed the defense, or about 73 if you believed the prosecution.

In 1994, when Marvin was thirty-two years old, an anonymous informer told the police that Marvin was a drug dealer. When the informer was found dead, Marvin and another man, Terry Lewis, were arrested and charged with the murder. It was clear from other eyewitness accounts that the

MARVIN WILSON AFTER HIS ARREST FOR MURDER.

murderer had been either Marvin or Terry. There was no forensic or other evidence pointing to which of the two men actually had committed the murder.

The question for the jury was which man had pulled the trigger. The jury decided Marvin was the murderer. The evidence against him was mostly the testimony of Terry's wife, who told the court she overheard Marvin confess to the crime.

A jury has a right to believe whomever they want, and in this case, the jury believed that Terry's wife was telling the truth and Marvin was lying.

As a result of her testimony, Terry was given life in prison.

Marvin was sentenced to die.

• • • •

The United States Supreme Court has said that executing people with an IQ below 70 is unconstitutional because it is cruel to execute a person who may not have a complete understanding of right and wrong, and who might not even understand why he is dying. Texas law forbids the execution of anyone whose IQ is under 70. So the question of whether Marvin's IQ was above or below 70 was an important one—his very life depended on it.

Family members testified that Marvin showed serious mental limitations beginning in childhood. His cousin said, "The other kids in school would always call Marvin a dummy." According to the defense, Marvin couldn't use a phone book, couldn't match his socks, and didn't understand what a bank account was for. He had been known to fasten his belt to the point of nearly cutting off his circulation. When Marvin's son was born, Marvin began sucking his own thumb.

The prosecution argued that his intelligence was over 70 because the nature of his crime—murdering an informant—showed intelligence. The prosecution won.

Marvin Wilson was not able to file one of his appeals because he missed the deadline and the court refused to allow the appeal to be filed late. The court recognized that the fault lay with the lawyer representing Marvin, and also recognized that the result was harsh, particularly with a death penalty case. However, certain deadlines, according to the court, must be strictly enforced.

A prisoner who was able to read law books and understand the deadlines would have had one more chance to appeal.

Marvin died by lethal injection at 6:27 p.m. on August 7, 2012.

Marvin's case drew national attention because of the fear that he died not because he was guilty but because a more sophisticated accomplice was able to convince a jury that Marvin was the guilty one.

• • • •

Just as there is no perfect person, there is no perfect system. At each stage along the process of arresting and convicting criminals, people have to make decisions, and each person — being human — is prone to make mistakes. The process often starts when someone calls to report a crime. That person forms an opinion of what happened and relays that opinion to the police. Next, a dispatcher must decide whether to send a police officer. When the police arrive, they have to make decisions, including whether to arrest someone, and if so, who. After an arrest, a prosecutor must make decisions, including how much priority to give each case.

Human beings have biases — inclinations toward certain ideas that may or may not be correct. For example, though studies show that jurors take their task seriously, even well-meaning jurors have biases. In the words of one psychologist who studied cases in which jurors reached decisions that were contrary to the evidence: "An individual views others as belonging to either their own group (the in-group) or another group (the out-group.) Such distinctions are based on many dimensions, including race, religion, gender, age, ethnic background, occupation, and income."

At the conclusion of the murder trial of two boys accused of killing their parents, some jurors confided that they did not believe the boys had committed the murder because "the boys looked like nice young men."

Retribution requires that people get what they deserve, but in a system run by human beings, how can we be sure the people who are punished deserve it and those not punished deserve not to be punished? If the punishments meted out by the courts were not so harsh—if there were no death penalty, for example, and if nobody served long prison sentences, and if lives were not ruined and families not destroyed as a result of severe punishments—the flaws in the criminal justice system would not matter so much. We would shrug and say, "People make mistakes. To err, after all, is human." But in our criminal justice system, a human error can result in the killing or imprisonment of an innocent person.

Just as we can never be sure everyone who has been punished got what he or she deserved, it is impossible to punish *all* wrongdoing. Imagine what would happen if every single wrongdoing worthy of punishment were criminalized and every person who committed a crime were punished by the government. As matters stand, remember, one in thirty-four Americans is serving some form of sentence. Imagine how many prisons would need to be built if every single behavior deserving punishment were criminalized and every crime resulted in a conviction.

So, while the theory of retribution has a lot of commonsense appeal, it also has flaws and shortcomings. If we can never be sure that people walking free are less guilty than people in jail, it cannot be said that the criminal justice system gives people what they deserve and restores moral balance.

CHAPTER 8

DETERRENCE, OR A WARNING TO ALL

Deterrence is the theory that people won't commit crimes—or they will be less likely to commit crimes—if they know they will be punished. Deterrence is based on the assumption, among others, that people know what is legal and what is not. Just for a moment, imagine James Rogers at the bank. The teller puts down a large stack of money and James has a split second to decide what to do. People are in line behind him. The teller considers their transaction finished. What should he do? Should he pick up the money and leave? Or should he say, "Hey, I think you made a mistake!"

A great many people, even those who consider themselves to be honest, law-abiding citizens, might feel tempted to keep the money.

Those who favor deterrence assume that something like this will go through the mind of someone in that position: "It's really tempting to take all this money, but if I take it, I'll be violating that law that defines bank robbery as walking out of the bank with more than a thousand dollars belonging to the bank. So I'd better not do it."

The first problem with deterrence is that most people wouldn't know that taking advantage of a teller's mistake can be considered bank robbery with a penalty of prison time.

Most people are likely to know that taking advantage of someone's mistake is not honest, but dishonesty is not necessarily criminal. Moreover, nobody could be expected to know that if the amount carried away is more than $1,000, the punishment becomes much harsher.

So a person might think, "I shouldn't keep this. It's wrong," but having no idea it was a felony with a prison sentence, she might keep it anyway, figuring, "It was the teller's mistake, not mine."

• • • •

There's a second problem with the theory of deterrence: It works only if everyone is able to make rational decisions.

Nicholas Horner, a husband and father, served as a soldier in Iraq. He was awarded multiple medals for his military service, including a combat action badge. As a result of his experiences in combat, he developed post-traumatic stress disorder (PTSD), a kind of anxiety that occurs after a person has experienced a deeply traumatic event. PTSD causes actual physical changes in the body, including changes in hormones and chemicals that carry information to the nerves. Soldiers returning from battle often have PTSD. Time in prison has been known to cause it as well.

Nicholas was discharged for PTSD with a 50 percent disability, which was later increased to 100 percent. After he returned home, his family said he was changed. He was fearful and jumpy and inclined to commit violence. He asked to be put into the hospital because he was, in his words, a "walking shell," but the hospital would not admit him.

Three weeks after he had asked to be admitted to the hospital, he went on a rampage in his hometown and killed

72

NICHOLAS HORNER WITH HIS DAUGHTER.

two innocent people and wounded another. The people he killed did nothing at all to provoke him. Later he was unable to recall the incident.

His murder trial lasted six days. Much of the evidence concerned the harmful impact of his military service, which included two tours in Iraq and one in Kuwait. His lawyers wanted to put forward an insanity defense, but the court would not allow it when the diagnosis was PTSD. His lawyers, therefore, focused on his diagnosis of PTSD, hoping to convince the jury that he had committed the violence because of the disorder. Succeeding on such a defense would have meant a conviction of second-degree murder instead of first-degree. The difference is that first-degree murder carries a possible death penalty, while second-degree murder means a maximum sentence of life in prison.

Under the law, what mattered was whether he knew what he did was wrong. The prosecution's argument was that he knew killing innocent people who hadn't provoked him

was wrong, so, under the law, he was guilty.

The jury found him guilty and sentenced him to life in prison.

Nicholas might have known that murdering innocent people was wrong. But if the trauma he suffered in combat changed the way his brain works, actually altering the chemistry of his brain so that he could not make rational decisions, deterrence simply could not work.

• • • •

Two high school seniors brought guns to school on April 29, 1999, and went on a shooting rampage, killing twelve students and one teacher at Columbine High School in Columbine, Colorado. They wounded twenty-one others. There have been other such massacres, some even bloodier, including the more recent slaughter of twenty children and six adult staff members at Sandy Hook Elementary School in Connecticut on December 14, 2012.

Almost always, the shooter ends up dead, either because someone else killed him to end the rampage or because the shooter was on a suicide mission.

Investigations into the most horrific of crimes generally show that the killers had deep-seated mental illnesses, such as sociopathy.

Sociopathy is a personality disorder. Sociopaths entirely lack the ability to take responsibility for their actions. They lack a sense of moral responsibility or social conscience. Frequently they are driven to act in antisocial ways and feel no remorse when they cause pain.

A psychopath has a similar disorder. Psychopaths have shallow emotions, including a lack of empathy for others. While not all psychopaths are criminals—many lead productive lives—some are aggressive and show no remorse for their actions.

Most mental illnesses can be treated, but according to Professor David Eagleman of the Baylor College of Medicine, there is no effective treatment for a psychopath. This is partly because a psychopath's brain is different from that of a non-psychopathic person. The major difference is smaller size of the part of the brain that registers emotion. The condition is physical, and a part of who the psychopath is.

The boys who went on the shooting spree in Columbine knew they would die but didn't care. A person on a suicide mission doesn't care in the least if he faces harsh punishment. Moreover, if a person has such a deep-seated mental illness that he does not experience what's considered normal emotions, the threat of deterrence will not work.

• • • • •

Charles Whitman was a twenty-five-year-old graduate student when he lugged a trunk of rifles up a tower on the campus of the University of Texas on August 1, 1966. He was a former marine, so, like Nicholas Horner, he'd honed his shooting skills in the military.

Charles went on a shooting rampage, killing fourteen

students and terrifying the entire campus. During the weeks leading up to the killings, he'd been complaining of headaches and an altered mental state. Before climbing the tower, he wrote a suicide note that read, "I do not really understand myself these days. I am supposed to be an average reasonable and intelligent young man. However lately (I cannot recall when it started) I have been a victim of many irrational thoughts." He also wrote, "After my death, I wish that an autopsy would be performed on me to see if there was any visible physical disorder."

An autopsy is a medical procedure done on a body after death, usually to determine the actual cause of death.

After Charles Whitman's death, an autopsy revealed

CHARLES WHITMAN KILLED FOURTEEN PEOPLE AT THE UNIVERSITY OF TEXAS IN 1966. IT WAS LATER DISCOVERED THAT HE HAD A BRAIN TUMOR THAT AFFECTED HIS ABILITY TO REGULATE HIS EMOTIONS.

that he had a brain tumor pressing against the part of the brain believed to be responsible for regulating emotions. By his own admission, his thinking had been disordered and irrational in the weeks leading to his killing spree. The theory of deterrence, remember, is based on the idea that people can make rational decisions—but if someone has something so deeply wrong with his brain that he cannot think rationally, the threat of harsh punishment may not deter him from committing a crime.

• • • •

A forty-year-old teacher in Virginia suddenly began exhibiting criminal behavior. He was convicted of child abuse and put into a rehabilitation program. He continued exhibiting criminal behavior in this program, however, so he was imprisoned. A brain scan revealed that he had a large brain tumor displacing the frontal lobe of his brain—the part of the brain that helps a person control his behavior.

People with damage to the frontal lobe of their brain understand that what they are doing is wrong, but they lack the ability to control themselves. The law recognizes insanity as a defense, but only if a person was unable to understand at the time that their behavior was wrong. Frontal lobe brain damage, therefore, often doesn't prevent a person from being convicted of a crime. In fact, one researcher estimated that up to 94 percent of people convicted of murder have some form of brain dysfunction.

If the most dangerous crimes are committed by psychopaths and people on suicide missions or other people with something just plain wrong with their brain, deterrence as a preventive approach fails in the crimes from which we most need protection.

• • • •

In 1992 and 1993, two girls were murdered in separate incidents in California.

First, on June 30, 1992, Kimber Reynolds, eighteen years old, was out in Fresno having dessert with some friends. As she left the restaurant, two men came by on a motorbike and tried to grab her purse. She fought to hold on to it. One of her attackers, a man named Joe Davis, shot her in the head and killed her.

Then, on October 1, 1993, twelve-year-old Polly Klaas of Petaluma, California, invited two friends for a slumber party. Late in the evening, a man entered her bedroom with a knife. He tied up her two friends and kidnapped Polly. For two months, four thousand people helped search for her. When Richard Allen Davis (no relation to Joe Davis) was arrested for a routine parole violation on November 30, 1993, he was identified as Polly's kidnapper by his palm print. He confessed and led police to Polly's body. He said he strangled her from behind with a piece of cloth.

Richard Allen Davis was tried and found guilty and sentenced to death. He is still on death row at San Quentin State Prison in Marin County, California.

Kimber's father vowed to do something to prevent other senseless murders. What particularly enraged him was that both of the murderers—Joe Davis and Richard Allen Davis—had prior convictions and were out on parole when they committed murder.

He led a movement to pass tougher criminal laws to

make sure that repeat offenders would not be able to continue committing crimes. The law he spearheaded was called Three Strikes. The idea was that after three strikes, you get life in prison. No exceptions.

California's Three Strikes law has been widely hailed as the toughest in the nation. In passing it, one lawmaker said the law was not only intended to keep dangerous criminals off the streets, but was a move toward "zero tolerance" for crime. Three Strikes was widely supported by the public and politicians of both major parties. One rationale for tough laws is that deterrence requires harsh penalties. If a penalty is too low, a person may decide to take his chances. Those opposed to the law said it was too extreme and came from public panic rather than rational policymaking.

During the first five years after the law was passed, the crime rate in California dropped by 26.9 percent, translating into 815,000 fewer crimes.

MURDER RATES (IN YEARS STATISTICS ARE AVAILABLE)			
	CALIFORNIA	NEW YORK	NATION AS A WHOLE
1990	3,553	2,262	9.3
1993	4,096	1,927	9.5
1994	3,703		9
1995			8.2
1998	2,171	628	6.3
2001	2,206		5.6
2006	2,485		5.7
2009	1,972		5
2011	1,792		4.7
2012		419	

Given that the murder rate in California dropped approximately by half since the law was passed, Three Strikes seems to have succeeded in preventing crime. However, places that did not enact a three strikes law, such New York, had a similar drop in murder rates. In fact, New York City showed an even more dramatic drop in the murder rate during the same period, without passing the same sort of harsh law.

Even more startling, the overall murder rates across the entire United States dropped dramatically between 1990 and 2012. Though the murder rate in California did indeed go down, the murder rate went down everywhere in the country, and in places that did not enact three strikes laws, the murder rate went down even more.

How can that be?

Any answer must be based on speculation. It is always difficult to say why something happens, or what causes what. When the national crime rate decreases steadily over a long period, figuring out precisely what is causing the drop is extremely difficult because there are so many different possible factors. What all of this suggests, however, is that harsh punishment does not necessarily deter crime.

• • • •

Another facet of deterrence is the idea that prison will teach someone a lesson: Criminals will learn, from harsh punishment, that it is better not to commit crimes. But punishment won't help a person learn if he or she has something wrong with his or her brain and cannot learn.

Recidivism is a term that refers to lapsing back into crime. A high recidivism rate means lots of people continue to commit crimes even after serving a prison sentence.

Statistics show that while the overall crime rate went down from 1990 to 2012, the recidivism rate in the United States remained high even after tough laws were passed. Almost half of the prisoners released from prison committed a second crime and were sent back to prison. More than 43 percent of prisoners released in 2004 were back behind bars within three years.

Researchers and social scientists put forward various theories for why there are so many repeat offenders. One cites the high level of violence in prisons, including unprovoked attacks on inmates from guards, which can "harden" a criminal, making him more likely to commit future crimes. A man in prison is eighteen times more likely to experience violence (such as being attacked by another inmate or by a guard) than a man outside prison. A woman has a 27 percent higher chance of being attacked in prison than in the outside world. The question then becomes is there a point at which inflicting pain on people will make them more likely to commit violence later?

Other researchers conclude that people in prison, particularly those guilty of minor or petty offenses, learn from more experienced inmates how to commit different types of crimes. Further studies show that cutting off prisoners' ties to their families and communities hardens them and makes them resentful and more likely to commit crimes.

Additionally, a person released from prison can have extreme difficulty finding a respectable job. If, like James Rogers, he is convicted of a felony, he carries the stigma for life. Convictions are public information. Felonies—which are particularly serious crimes such as murder, arson, and robbery—must be disclosed on job applications, so a felon will have a hard time finding work, possibly for the rest of his life. A person is more likely to commit additional crimes if denied a way to earn a living.

Most states restrict the rights of felons to vote in elections after they are released. Some states take away the right to vote for the remainder of the felon's life. Other states allow a person convicted of a felony to regain the right to vote depending on the nature of the crime and the length of time since the person's release from prison.

People who cannot work or vote, and are barred from participating in society in basic ways, will have even less incentive to follow rules—and thus the cycle continues.

If harsh punishment does not deter crime, and if the recidivism rate remains high despite harsh punishment, harsh punishment becomes difficult to justify.

· · · ·

Hand in hand with deterrence is the theory of incapacitation, which puts forth the idea that the way to reduce crime is to put criminals in jail so that they cannot commit any more crimes. Like other theories of punishment, this one appeals to common sense. A person cannot commit more crimes if she is in jail.

Incapacitation has many of the same problems as deterrence, and there is much overlap in both justifications for punishment. In fact, one of the purposes of California's Three Strikes law and others like it was to incapacitate criminals. Kimber's father, after her murder, spearheaded the law precisely so that repeat offenders can't get out of jail and commit more crimes.

Keeping everyone who commits a single crime in jail for a long time might reduce the amount of crime. But keeping someone who commits a crime in jail in order to prevent her from committing another crime means the sentence depends on the probability that she will commit another crime rather than on the severity of what she already did. Suppose a person has kleptomania—a psychiatric condition in which he impulsively steals. But suppose too that the person steals only very small items. Keeping a petty thief in jail to prevent additional crimes means the punishment would not fit the crime.

Moreover, the cost of imprisoning someone is about $40,000 per year, depending on the state, which means both deterrence and incapacitation cost taxpayers enormous amounts of money. This raises the question of whether any of the benefits are worth the cost.

In 2010, the California state auditor reported that as of 2008, the Three Strikes law had cost the state of California an extra $19.2 billion because of how many more people California imprisoned as a result of the law. The $19.2 billion was in addition to the money already being spent on prisons and law enforcement.

The United States, overall, spends $60 billion a year on prisons, parole, and probation. Critics of the tough-on-crime laws point out that the $60 billion for prisons takes money away from schools, medical care, and services for families in need. This is a lot of money to spend if harsh punishments have limited benefits and may, in fact, do more harm than good.

CHAPTER 9

THE CONVEYOR BELT OF JUSTICE

When a parent punishes a child, or a school punishes a student, there is a human dimension to the punishment. Not all parents do a good job with giving punishments or reprimands, but generally—in a loving family—the parent knows and understands the child and is acting in the child's best interest to try to teach him or her proper behavior through consequences.

A school, too, knows the child. The teachers and principals in good schools ask questions such as "Why is the child behaving this way? Are there things we can do to help the child behave better before we resort to more extreme measures, which may have a lifelong impact on the child?"

Our criminal justice system is a bureaucracy managed in a methodical, impersonal way. If a society is going to put millions of people in jail, it must develop a highly efficient criminal justice system. The final problem with the crime control model comes from this very efficiency.

A police department that frequently arrested people who were then proven innocent would be considered an inefficient police department. A prosecutor who was continually losing the cases she brought to trial would be considered a bad prosecutor. People would wonder why she wasn't screening her cases better. People would wonder why the police weren't doing a better job with their investigations. Moreover, arresting and charging innocent people with crimes is a major disruption in their lives, not to mention a source of humiliation and embarrassment. Bringing innocent people to trial harms the very people the criminal justice system is seeking to protect.

The ideal, therefore, is for police departments to develop such good investigatve procedures that the innocent are quickly screened out and the only people arrested and brought to trial are those the police and prosecutors are fairly certain are guilty. This is also cost-effective: It is much easier and more efficient for police officers to get to the truth during pre-arrest investigations and questioning. Trials are expensive.

Prosecutors, for this reason, have a lot of discretion in which cases they will prosecute. If they believe a person is innocent, even if someone is accusing that person of a crime, they drop the charges and refuse to bring him to trial, because doing so would be a waste of taxpayer money.

Plea bargains make the system work even more efficiently. With a plea bargain, there is no trial at all—the accused agrees to plead guilty so that a trial can be avoided. There is a reason these are called plea *bargains*. Once a person has been charged with a crime, the prosecutor offers him or her a deal: If the accused will plead guilty, the prosecutor will lessen the charge so the accused can receive a lighter punishment.

According to the United States Bureau of Justice and estimates from other organizations, 90 to 95 percent of all criminal cases are decided by means of a plea bargain.

Tough penalties help a prosecutor convince suspects to plead guilty. Suppose, for example, a woman in 1960 was caught smoking marijuana. The 1952 Boggs Act and the 1956 Narcotics Control Act made first-time use of marijuana a crime punishable by a minimum of two to ten years in prison and a fine of up to $20,000.

Suppose this woman had a few enemies who planted marijuana on her property and called the police. The police questioned everyone and believed the informants. The prosecutor, after examining the evidence, also believed them but would prefer to have the accused plead guilty rather than bring the case to trial. Suppose then the prosecutor said, "If you go to trial and lose, I will ask for the maximum penalty of ten years and a $20,000 fine. If you plead guilty to a lesser offense instead, you will get only six months in the local jail."

What would you do? Take a chance?

In fact, most defendants accept the plea bargain partly because going to trial is perceived as risky. It is impossible to predict what witnesses will say, or what a jury will do. Moreover, the truth is not always easy to discover. Even eyewitness testimony can be unreliable — two eyewitnesses can see the same event differently. And of course, not all eyewitnesses are truthful. In short, the decision of any jury and court depends on many factors that are out of the control of the accused.

The efficiency required to imprison millions of people has been likened to an industrial assembly line, or conveyor belt, that quickly and effectively moves a product from beginning to end.

In the same way, a quality police department with

state-of-the-art investigative and evidence-gathering techniques swiftly arrests those who are likely to be guilty, and releases those likely innocent, and so these police officers arrest and charge only those they truly believe are guilty.

A well-organized police department with top-notch investigative tools creates an interesting situation: If the police investigations are thorough and prosecutors are good at their jobs, by the time a person is charged with a crime, there is a very strong likelihood that the person is guilty.

Why is this a problem?

If the criminal justice system becomes so efficient that a person charged with a crime and brought to court is most likely guilty, what happens to the guarantee that every person charged with a crime is innocent until proven guilty in court? By the time a person is arrested, questioned by the police, charged by a prosecutor, and brought to court, wouldn't there be a *presumption of guilt* in the minds of the public and even the jurors? In the case of plea bargains, there isn't even a trial with a jury, after all. The person's guilt or innocense is essentially decided by police and prosecutors.

Allowing police and prosecutors to decide guilt and innocence is a cost-effective way of allowing large numbers of people to be arrested, charged, convicted, and imprisoned. But the question is whether it is a good idea to give too much power to the police.

PART THREE:

DUE PROCESS AND THE PRESUMPTION
OF INNOCENCE

As everyone knows, a person accused of a crime is innocent until proven guilty.

You might assume that such a basic guarantee was written in the United States Constitution. As a matter of fact, it isn't. Neither is it in the Declaration of Independence, nor any of our country's founding documents.

The concept of innocent until proven guilty has roots so deep in English common law, the framers of the Constitution may have taken the guarantee so much for granted that they just didn't include it.

The first ten amendments, also called the Bill of Rights, added in 1791, offer many of the personal freedoms we take for granted. The Fourth Amendment guarantees the right to be free from unreasonable searches and seizures—even though the Fourth Amendment does not explain what is meant by "reasonable."

The Fifth Amendment says a person may not be called to answer for a crime without first being indicted by a grand jury, and does not have to be a witness against himself—which means the right to remain silent—and cannot be deprived of life, liberty, or property without due process of law. The Constitution, however, does not explain what it is meant by "due process of law."

The Sixth Amendment gives an accused person the right to a speedy trial by an impartial jury, and the right to confront witnesses and compel witnesses to court.

It's easy to think from all this that a person accused of a crime has a lot of rights and constitutional protections. Nothing to worry about.

There is one hitch.

The Bill of Rights applies only to the federal government. A federal government cannot take a person's liberty, property, or life without due process and all the other guarantees.

Most crimes, however, are prosecuted at the state and local levels. The Bill of Rights says nothing at all about what local police and local courts can't do or must do.

For much of our history—up until the Civil War—states pretty much did whatever they wanted, which was why some states allowed slavery and others did not. Part of the reason for the Civil War was to decide whether states could act as their own separate legal entities, or whether state governments, like the federal government, had to guarantee all people basic rights and freedoms.

As a result of the Civil War, two amendments were added to the Constitution. The Thirteenth Amendment abolished slavery, and the Fourteenth Amendment required the states to give all citizens equal protection of the laws and due process of law. Section 1 of the Fourteenth Amendment guarantees all people equal protection of the laws, and due process of law before the government can deprive them of life, liberty, or property.

That's it. The Fourteenth Amendment says nothing about the right to a speedy trial, the right to remain silent, the right to a lawyer, or much of anything at all specific. The Fourteenth Amendment guarantees only equal protection of the laws and due process of law and offers no definition of what these things require.

The Civil War did not end the debate about how much states should be allowed to decide for themselves how they wanted to govern and live, and to what extent states must conform to national standards. For decades after the Civil War, the understanding was that each state could set its own standards and interpret for itself what is meant by equal protection and due process.

Then, in the 1950s, the United States Supreme Court began telling states what due process under the Fourteenth Amendment required—and criminal law has never been the same since.

An illustration in *Harper's Weekly* magazine showing the scene in the House of Representatives when the Thirteenth Amendment was passed.

CHAPTER 10

DOLLY MAPP AND UNREASONABLE SEARCHES

A bomb exploded on the front porch of a home in a suburb of Cleveland, Ohio, at three a.m. on May 20, 1957. The home belonged to Donald King, a man with ties to illegal gambling operations. During the investigation into the bombing, the police received an anonymous telephone tip that Virgil Ogletree, a key suspect in the bombing, was hiding in the home of a woman named Dollree (Dolly) Mapp.

Three days later, Cleveland police officers arrived at Dolly's house. When the doorbell rang, Dolly opened a window and asked what they wanted. One of the officers

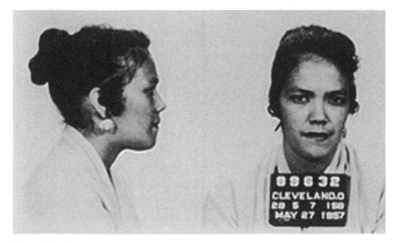

Dolly Mapp's case set in motion our laws governing what law enforcement officials can search and how.

said they wanted to question her but wouldn't offer any details.

She told the police she wanted to call her lawyer. With the door still locked and the officers on her front porch, she called her lawyer. Her lawyer was not available, but his partner, Walter Greene, told her not to let the police inside unless they had a search warrant and let her read it.

The police didn't have a warrant, so she wouldn't let them in. They remained outside on her porch for three hours, during which time four more officers arrived. One of the police officers kicked Dolly's front door and demanded to be let in. Dolly still refused to open the door, so one of the officers broke the glass in the door and reached inside to unlock it so the other officers could enter.

Walter Greene, Dolly's lawyer, arrived just in time to see the officers push their way into the house. Dolly, who was coming down the stairs, demanded to see their search warrant. One of the officers held up a piece of paper and said, "Here is the search warrant." Dolly asked to see it, but the officer refused.

Dolly grabbed the paper from the officer's hand and shoved it down the front of her dress. The officer seized her, reached into her dress, and grabbed the paper. He pulled her arm, twisted it back, and roughly handcuffed her to the bed. She cried out because he was hurting her.

Walter Greene tried to enter the home, but the officers would not let him in, and would not let him talk to Dolly.

The police officers searched the entire house. They rifled through private papers and photo albums. They found the suspect they were looking for, Virgil Ogletree. They also found a gun, several pornographic books, and evidence of illegal gambling. The police confiscated the items and arrested Dolly.

At the police station, the police questioned Virgil Ogletree but decided he had nothing to do with the bombing after all, so they let him go.

Dolly, however, was charged with possessing pornographic books and gambling paraphernalia. The gambling charge was a misdemeanor that was handled quickly. Dolly was brought to trial and was found not guilty.

Possession of pornography, however, was a serious offense in 1957 in Ohio. In fact, possession of pornography was a felony, and under Ohio law required more complicated procedures. Four months after her arrest, she was charged with possessing pornography. Initially she pleaded guilty, but she changed her plea to not guilty and demanded a jury trial.

The lawyer she hired to defend her, Alexander Kearns, filed a motion to suppress the evidence, arguing that evidence obtained without a valid search warrant should not be used against Dolly in court.

But under the law as it stood in 1957, the motion to suppress the evidence was bound to fail, because the Fourth Amendment, which guaranteed a person the right to be free from unreasonable searches and seizures, applied only to the federal government and the search had been done by local police.

Dolly's lawyer, of course, knew this. But he had to argue something in her defense. She'd been caught red-handed with the pornographic material in her house. She was the only adult living there, so the evidence was compelling. The only thing he could really do was try to argue that the evidence against her was gathered illegally and therefore should not be used in court.

Although the police never put forward any indication that they had a valid search warrant, the trial court denied the motion on the grounds that the evidence itself had not been taken from her person by force. Dolly was convicted of possessing pornography and sentenced to prison for at least one but not more than seven years.

She appealed to the Ohio Supreme Court, which ruled that the evidence was admissible on the grounds that it had not been taken from Dolly's "person by the use of brutal or offensive force."

Her case went all the way to the United States Supreme Court. In its ruling in Dolly's case, it gave an interpretation of the Fourth and Fourteenth Amendments that remains controversial to this day. The Supreme Court said that the specific protections given in the Fourth Amendment, including the right to be free from unreasonable searches and seizures, applies to the states as well as the federal government through the Fourth Amendment.

The problem was how to enforce the Fourteenth Amendment. What would prevent local governments, police departments, and courts from simply doing what they wanted and later simply saying, "Oops, we shouldn't have done that!"

The Supreme Court decided there must be consequences if police officers overstep an individual's right to be free from unreasonable search and seizure. But who should — or could — monitor the police?

Because the heart of the matter was interpreting the Constitution, it seemed to the Supreme Court that the lower courts should have the task of monitoring police departments. And the way to do that, the Court decided, was through what is called the exclusionary rule. Under the exclusionary rule, any evidence procured in violation of a person's constitutional rights is inadmissible in court. If the police search a person without enough cause, and find evidence of guilt, the evidence is not admissible in court and the person cannot be convicted.

Some people thought that the Supreme Court—a federal institution—was reaching beyond the wording of the Constitution and fashioning an interpretation that the original framers didn't intend: according to many, the framers of the Constitution were interested in limiting the power and reach of the federal government to strengthen local governments.

Others agreed with the ruling, believing that the Fourteenth Amendment, which guarantees a person due process of the law, should not allow police to behave in the manner they did when they forcibly entered Dolly's house.

The exclusionary rule is controversial also because it means that actual evidence that might prove a person's guilt sometimes cannot be used in court. Opponents feel that this allows guilty people to walk away free simply because the police blundered. Those who support the rule say the most important consideration is making sure that police officers respect the Constitution, and the only real way to do that is not to allow illegally gathered evidence to be used in court.

Once the Supreme Court decided that the evidence

against Dolly had been obtained by the police in violation of her constitutional rights, and once the court applied the exclusionary rule, there was no longer any evidence against her that could be used in court.

Without evidence, she could not be convicted.

Her conviction was therefore overturned, and she walked away free.

CHAPTER II

THE RIGHT TO COUNSEL

Fifty-one-year-old Clarence Earl Gideon was arrested on June 3, 1961, and charged with burglarizing the Bay Harbor Poolroom in Panama City, Florida. The crime was a felony.

Clarence—a frail man with white hair—had a long criminal history, and had been in and out of prisons much of his life. He was first arrested at the age of fourteen for burglarizing a county store for clothes. He was caught the next day wearing the clothing he had stolen and was sent to a juvenile "reformatory." Later he said of all the prisons he'd been in, that was the worst, and he carried permanent scars from the whippings he received. He was released at age twenty-two, in the middle of the Great Depression. He found a job in a shoe factory, but he was arrested again for stealing government property and sentenced to three years in federal prison. When he got out, he worked some more and saved a little money, which he sent to his parents to help them buy a house. He was arrested several more times over the years, each time for burglary.

At the time of his 1961 arrest, he'd been convicted of four felonies. If he was convicted of burglarizing the Bay Harbor Poolroom, it would be his fifth.

Clarence pled not guilty.

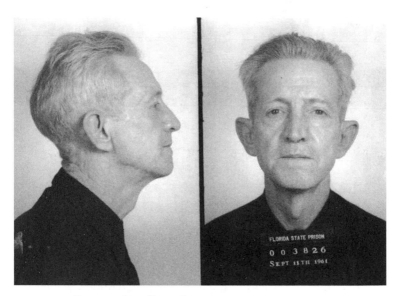

CLARENCE EARL GIDEON'S CASE HELPED SHAPE THE RIGHTS
OF THOSE ACCUSED OF CRIMES TODAY.

He was brought to trial on August 4, 1961. The judge asked him if he was ready to go to trial and he said he was not.

"Why aren't you ready?" asked the judge.

"I have no counsel," said Clarence.

"Why do you not have counsel? Did you not know your trial was scheduled for today?"

Clarence said he knew the trial was scheduled for that day—but he had no counsel because he couldn't afford it. He demanded the court appoint him a lawyer.

The law as it stood in 1961, however, did not require a court-appointed lawyer for a person who could not afford one. The Sixth Amendment of the Constitution provides that criminal defendants have the right to counsel to assist in their defense, but it does not specifically say that if you can't afford one, a lawyer will be provided free of charge.

Moreover, the Sixth Amendment, as mentioned, applied only to the federal government, and Clarence was in state court. Florida law required criminal defendants to be given a lawyer only if they were being charged with a crime that could be punished with the death penalty.

Clarence Gideon, however, had the firm — and many at the time believed irrational — belief that the United States Constitution entitled him to have a lawyer even if he couldn't afford one.

The judge denied Clarence's request for court-appointed counsel, and the trial went forward. The prosecution brought in two witnesses against Clarence. The first was Henry Cook of Panama City. Henry and Clarence knew each other. Henry testified that on the morning of June 3, he saw Clarence come out of the Bay Harbor Poolroom with a pint of wine in his hand, make a telephone call at the corner phone booth, wait, then get into a taxi. After following Clarence to the corner, he went back to the poolroom and saw it had been broken into. The front was off the cigarette machine and the money box was on the pool table.

Clarence, representing himself, cross-examined Henry. He asked such questions as what Henry was doing outside the poolroom at five-thirty. Henry testified that he had been out all night dancing.

The other witness for the prosecution was Ira Strickland Jr., manager of the Bay Harbor Poolroom. Ira testified that he had locked the place up at about twelve the night before. In the morning, he found that someone had smashed the window and broken into the cigarette machine and jukebox. The culprit had taken coins, but Ira didn't know how many.

Clarence called a few witnesses in his defense, including the police officer and his own landlady, who testified that he frequently left early in the morning to use the corner payphone so he wouldn't wake the others in the house. She also testified that she had never seen him intoxicated.

Clarence then made a closing argument to the jury, stressing that he was innocent.

The jury found Clarence guilty.

The judge delayed sentencing him for three weeks to get a report on his past history. On August 25, without any further proceedings, the judge sentenced Clarence to the maximum sentence of five years in prison. Clarence was sent to the Florida state prison in Raiford, Florida.

• • • •

Clarence went to prison with a furious and passionate belief that he was the victim of a great injustice inflicted upon him by the state of Florida.

While there, presumably with law books checked out from the prison library, he obtained a copy of the Supreme Court rules and handwrote his own appeal on lined paper provided by the prison.

"The question is very simple," he wrote to the Supreme Court. "I requested the court to appoint me [an] attorney and the court refused."

The Supreme Court agreed to hear Clarence's case, and immediately appointed a top constitutional lawyer to represent him.

On Monday, March 18, 1963, almost two years after Clarence's trial, the Supreme Court handed down its decision. The court decided that the Fourteenth Amendment — which guarantees due process but doesn't mention right to counsel—requires state courts to provide lawyers for criminal defendants who cannot afford their own.

This was, to say the least, a *very* controversial opinion. Many felt that the financial burden on states would be too great. Paying for lawyers for everyone who can't afford one is enormously expensive. Critics of the opinion said taxpayers should not bear the burden of paying for lawyers to represent poor people. Those who hailed the decision as a step forward in securing personal liberty for all people felt that the system would not work if only the wealthy have lawyers.

Clarence's win in the Supreme Court did not mean he was free to walk out of prison. The ruling entitled him to a new trial, this time with a lawyer appointed by the court and paid for by the state of Florida.

To make sure Clarence had top-notch lawyers, the American Civil Liberties Union (ACLU) hired two lawyers to represent Clarence and sent them to Florida.

When everyone was gathered together in court, Clarence made the startling announcement that he didn't want the ACLU lawyers. He wanted a local lawyer. And he knew who he wanted: W. Fred Turner.

The judge excused the ACLU lawyers and appointed W. Fred Turner. The trial was rescheduled to give Fred time to prepare for the trial.

Fred prepared by spending a full day nosing around Bay Harbor, talking to people and familiarizing himself with the Bay Harbor Poolroom.

The case came to trial on August 8, 1963.

Henry Cook, the witness who claimed to have seen

Clarence walking from the poolroom on the morning of July 3, once again took the witness stand.

Fred asked Henry how he came to be in front of the poolroom at five a.m. Henry said the friends he had been with all night dropped him off. Fred then asked why his friends dropped him off at the poolroom instead of his own home, which was a few blocks away.

Henry said his plan had been to hang out for two hours waiting for the pool hall to open at seven.

Fred next produced a surprise witness who hadn't been called the first time around: J. D. Henderson, owner of the Bay Harbor Poolroom.

According to J. D. Henderson, Henry had been suspiciously hanging around the pool hall between five and seven a.m. J. D. Henderson also testified that twelve bottles of cola, twelve cans of beer, five dollars from the cigarette machine, and sixty dollars from the jukebox were stolen from the poolroom that night.

Henry's testimony that he saw Clarence leave the poolroom with a fifth of wine, make a phone call, and get into a cab did not account for what Clarence had done with all the beverages.

J. D. Henderson then testified that between eight and nine in the morning, Henry told him that he had been picked up by the police and questioned about the break-in. Henry also told J.D. that he had seen someone hanging around earlier, but he didn't know who it was. Then he said the person "looked like Clarence."

J.D. testified that sixty dollars had been stolen from the jukebox. When Clarence was arrested that morning, he had twenty-five dollars and twenty-eight cents, typical of his earnings from gambling.

In closing arguments, Clarence's lawyer presented his theory of the case: Henry Cook had been the one to break in and rob the poolroom. Henry saw Clarence make a phone call and get into a cab, so he pointed the finger at Clarence.

The jury was given their instructions: To convict Clarence, they had to believe beyond a reasonable doubt that he was guilty.

The jury deliberated for little more than an hour. They returned to the courtroom and announced their verdict.

Clarence Earl Gideon, they decided, was not guilty.

He walked out of the courtroom a free man.

Ever since the Supreme Court decided *Gideon v. Wainwright,* people who cannot afford lawyers are entitled to a lawyer appointed by the court and paid for by the government.

CHAPTER 12

CONVEYOR BELTS AND OBSTACLE COURSES

The Supreme Court did not stop with Dolly's and Clarence's cases. In another famous case, *Miranda v. Arizona,* the Supreme Court ruled that citizens must be informed of their rights prior to being questioned by police, and any evidence or statement obtained prior to a suspect being read his or her rights is inadmissible in court. This has led to what are commonly called the Miranda rights, which are "You have the right to remain silent. Anything you say can and will be used against you in a court of law. You have the right to an attorney. If you cannot afford one, one will be appointed for you."

The Supreme Court during this era also struck down segregation laws as unconstitutional, overruling *Plessy v. Ferguson,* and ended the common practice of allowing only whites to serve on juries — all in the name of equal protection and due process under the Fourteenth Amendment.

As a result, for anyone accused of a crime at the local or state level, the two most important words in the Constitution are, arguably, *due process.* Under the crime control model, remember, law and order is the ideal. According to the crime control view of criminal law, preventing crime is the most important function of criminal law, because without law and

MIRANDA RIGHTS

The famous Miranda case began on March 13, 1963, when police in Phoenix, Arizona, suspected Ernesto Miranda of kidnapping and attacking a ten-year-old girl. Ernesto Miranda was interrogated for two hours by the police. At the end of the interrogation, he signed a confession admitting the crime. At trial, he claimed that he had not confessed voluntarily. He was found guilty based on his confession. His case went to the United States Supreme Court, which reversed Ernesto's conviction on the grounds that nobody had informed him of his right to remain silent, or his right to a lawyer. Now, police have to read people their "Miranda rights" before questioning them.

order, you cannot have a free society and people cannot feel secure.

The opposing model, which has been called the due process model, takes a different view. Under the due process model, a free society means individuals have more personal liberty. People who value due process over crime control don't want it to be too easy for police to stop people unless the police have good reason to do so. They don't want the police to be entrusted with fact-finding. They want each person to have a jury trial, as guaranteed in the Constitution. In short, people who value due process over crime control believe that personal freedom comes from limiting government power, which means limiting police power and criminalizing fewer behaviors.

While the crime control method has been compared to a conveyor belt, the due process model has been compared to an obstacle course. The idea behind the due process model is to make it difficult, at each stage, for the government to deprive individuals of their property, their liberties, and their lives. The fear is that too efficient and robust a criminal justice system erodes the guarantee of innocent until proven guilty.

The two models present two different—and often conflicting—views of criminal justice.

CONCLUSION

THINKING LIKE A LAWYER

Criminal laws, like all laws, change and evolve. Some changes happen quickly, as when Congress passes an important law or the Supreme Court hands down a major decision. Other changes happen slowly, over time, as voters change their minds about how they feel regarding certain issues.

While some leaders are able to exert great influence to bring about change more quickly, ordinary citizens, too, create changes. They form committees, meet with their elected officials, or write letters expressing their views. They donate money to organizations trying to bring about the changes they'd like to see. They hand out flyers and talk to others, trying to persuade enough voters to agree with them. Some people make it their life's work to change the laws for the better.

With morally complex issues such as those involving criminal law, there are many theories and opinions and facts open to various interpretations, but relatively few truths on which everyone agrees.

In fact, everyone, it seems, has different ideas — and for democracy to work, all ideas can (and should!) be expressed and explored.

Clarence Darrow, a famous criminal defense lawyer,

believed that in a civilized society there should not be prisons at all. He also believed that the people in jail were not generally worse than the people not in jail—they were simply unluckier. He said, "It's not the bad people I fear so much as the good people. When a person is sure that he is good, he is nearly hopeless. He gets cruel. He believes in punishment."

CLARENCE DARROW

Thomas Szasz, a professor of psychiatry, believed punishment was justified because people should be held responsible for their own behavior. He believed people convicted of crimes should not be excused from punishment just because they supposedly have mental illnesses, because in his view, mental illnesses are largely myths and ways of letting people escape personal responsibility.

Fyodor Dostoyevsky, the nineteenth-century Russian author who wrote the famous novel *Crime and Punishment,* said that the degree of civilization in a society can be judged by entering its prisons.

Civil responsibility requires thinking about the laws and questioning whether they are right and how they can be improved. It requires seeing the complexity in seemingly simple questions such as "What is a crime?" and "Why do we punish?"

There is no perfect system—any system can be improved. In fact, for democracy to succeed, all citizens should become involved in the creation of policies and laws. Whatever improvements you believe can be made to the criminal justice system, the first step is to think critically about the laws and punishments imposed. Next test ideas through research and discuss your ideas with the people around you. This book is intended as a place to start.

GLOSSARY OF LEGAL TERMS

appeal: To ask a higher court to reverse the decision of a trial court.

appellate court: Any court that hears appeals from judgments and rulings of lower courts.

assault: A threat or attempt to strike another person, whether or not it is successful.

aggravated assault: The crime of physically attacking another person that results in serious harm.

battery: Intentionally striking someone, even if the injury is slight.

capital punishment: A death sentence.

case law: Reported decisions of appellate courts and other courts that offer new interpretations of the law.

caveat emptor: Latin for "Let the buyer beware."

civil law: Any body of laws that are not criminal, such as laws governing businesses, contracts, estates, wills, and family relationships such as marriage and divorces.

common law: The traditional unwritten law of England, based on custom and usage. Common law developed over hundreds of years in England before being passed into most states after the United States was formed. In some states today, the principles of common law are still so basic that they are applied without reference to written or specific case law.

constitutional: Does not violate rights given by the United States Constitution.

crime: An action or omission that constitutes an offense that may be prosecuted by the state and is punishable by law.

crime of opportunity: A crime committed without prior planning when the perpetrator sees an opportunity and takes it.

defense lawyer: In a criminal proceeding, the lawyer who represents the person accused of a crime.

domestic violence: The crime or problem of the physical beating of a domestic partner.

due process: The principle of fairness in legal proceedings, intended to safeguard the constitutional rights of citizens.

exclusionary rule: The rule that states that if law enforcement or government officials obtain evidence in violation of a citizen's constitutional rights, the evidence cannot be used in court.

felony: A crime serious enough to be punishable by prison time or death.

Fifth Amendment: The amendment guaranteeing a person accused of a crime such rights as the right to remain silent and the right to due process.

Fourteenth Amendment: The amendment added after the Civil War guaranteeing all citizens due process and equal protection of the laws.

Fourth Amendment: The amendment guaranteeing the right to be free from unreasonable search and seizure.

grand jury: A jury that hears evidence of criminal accusations in possible felonies and decides whether the prosecutor has enough evidence to charge the crime.

incapacitate: To deprive someone of an ability to do something.

indict: To charge a person with a crime.

larceny: The crime of theft of another person's property.

lawsuit: A legal action by one person against another, to be decided in court.

legislature: The lawmaking body of government.

liable: Responsible or obligated.

Miranda rights: The requirement set by the Supreme Court in *Miranda v. Arizona* that before arresting or questioning a suspect, the police must provide information about the constitutional right to remain silent and have a lawyer.

misdemeanor: A less serious crime punished by jail time of generally less than a year, or a fine.

morality crimes: Often called "victimless crimes," such as prostitution and recreational drug use; actions that are criminalized because they offend society's morals.

opinion: An appellate court decision containing the court's reasoning and how the court arrived at the decision.

plea bargain: A negotiation between the person accused and the prosecutor in which the person accused agrees to plead "guilty" in return for lesser punishment or dropping some of the charges, or some other concession from the prosecutor.

premeditate: To plan, or think out, ahead of time.

presumption of innocence: The idea that a person accused of a crime is innocent until proven guilty.

property crimes: Crimes of property, such as theft and vandalism.

prosecutor: The government lawyer in a criminal case who charges and prosecutes crimes.

punishment: A penalty imposed for wrongdoing.

recidivism: Relapsing into criminal behavior.

retribution: Punishment that is considered morally right because it is deserved.

segregation: Keeping people apart. Racial segregation is keeping people apart based on their race.

self-defense: A defense against a crime, using reasonable force to protect oneself or others.

settlement: An agreement reached by parties to a lawsuit which resolves the dispute prior to trial.

Sixth Amendment: The Amendment guaranteeing a person accused of a crime of several rights, including the right to a speedy and public trial and the right to a lawyer.

statutes: Written laws passed by Congress or a state legislature.

transferred intent: If, while acting in self-defense, someone injures or kills an innocent bystander but didn't intend to kill or injure that person, that person did not commit a crime.

United States Supreme Court: The highest court in the United States. The court that interprets the United States Constitution.

FOR FURTHER READING

Death Penalty Organizations and Sites: The University of Anchorage, Alaska, keeps a list of websites on both sides of the death penalty debate: justice.uaa.alaska.edu/death/procon.html.

For the **debate surrounding drug laws,** the Drug Policy Alliance (www.drugpolicy.com) and the Partnership at drugfree.org offer different views. The Drug Policy Alliance seeks to decriminalize drug use, believing that people should not be punished unless they harm others, and the Partnership at drugfree.org, in its concern for children, seeks a drug-free America and is opposed to legalizing drugs like marijuana.

Nolo: Law for All is an organization dedicated to providing low-cost legal information and help. Nolo maintains a list of articles on the criminal justice system: www.nolo.com/legal-encyclopedia/criminal-law.

The **Justice Policy Institute** is a nonprofit national organization dedicated to reducing the use of incarceration: www.justicepolicy.org/index.html.

Right on Crime, a conservative group that advocates both a "tough on crime" stance and a "tough on criminal justice spending" position: www.rightoncrime.com.

The **Three Strikes Reform** organization is an example of how a group of civil leaders and citizens got together to change and reform a law, in this case, California's Three Strikes law: www.fixthreestrikes.com/about.

For lesson plans and additional information, please see www.guilty-by-Teri-Kanefield.com.

ACKNOWLEDGMENTS

First thanks go to Professor Rory Little, teacher beyond compare and one of the authors of *Criminal Law: Cases and Materials* (with Saltzburg, Diamond, Morawetz, Kinports, and Little; Lexis Nexis, 2008), the textbook from which I first learned criminal law, and the text that inspired my selection of many of the cases discussed in this book. Thanks also to Betsy Wattenberg and Madeline Korn, who read early drafts and offered valuable suggestions; Carole Greeley, one of the smartest lawyers I know, who was kind enough to read the final draft and offer her thoughts; my editor Cynthia Platt, who believed in this book from the beginning and encouraged me to push beyond what was safe; Lisa Vega for an eye-catching cover. Thanks to the copyeditors, Alison Kerr Miller and Toni Rosenberg, both of whom have a very good eye for errors, and a very good ear for language. Finally, thanks to Andy, Dahvid, and Sabrina — and Joel, nine years old, who assured me that young readers will want to think about who we punish and why.

PHOTO CREDITS

NOTES

Introduction

page

ix   The term *crime control model* was first coined by Packer in "Two Models of the Criminal Process."

1. Crimes of Opportunity: Theft—or Good Luck?

7   "What if I found it": *Brooks v. State.*

8   "Is it worth twelve dollars" . . . "I'll take it": Verdi, "Charity Comes Out the Winner."

9   "stole" . . . "She just took the kid's word for it": Ibid.

    "I didn't steal the card . . . bargain all the time": Jones, "Inadvertent Disclosure of Privileged Information."

11   "If a bank sends you a check . . . live with its mistake": Verdi, "Charity Comes Out the Winner."

    "greatest baseball story of the spring": Downey, "Seller Beware in Card Games."

    "taffy pull": Verdi, "Charity Comes Out the Winner."

    "[Brian] was wrong . . . the Nolan Ryan rookie card": Jones, "Inadvertent Disclosure of Privileged Information and the Law of Mistake: Using Substantive Legal Principles to Guide Ethical Decision Making," *Emory Law Journal*, vol. 48, p. 1255, Fall 1999.

12   "What does it profit a boy . . . he gets a receipt?" As quoted by Trina Jones in "Inadvertent Disclosure of Privileged Information."

2. Another Kind of Bank Robbery

14   "They made one hundred and five . . . It's crooked": Serres, "Bank Fees Finagles?"

"The bottom line . . . a con job": West, "Two Maryland Victims of Banking System."

4. Race: Changing Attitudes and Laws

27–28   "Are you a colored man" . . . "retire to the colored car": Medley, *We as Freemen.*

32   "I'm for catching . . . concentration camps": Weber, "The Japanese Camps in California."

"Their racial . . . Japanese": Ibid.

36   "I would like to see . . . never happen to any American of any race, creed, or color": Fred T. Korematsu Institution for Civil Rights and Education, korematsuinstitute.org/institute/aboutfred.

5. Deciding What Is a Danger to Society

43–45   "The question is" to "governments are supreme": *State v. A. B. Rhodes.*

45   "divine laws" and "nature of thing": from *Bradwell v. The State.*

6. Killing Is a Crime, Except When It Isn't

51   "every night": Bronstein, "The Man Who Killed Osama bin Laden."

"Some killers . . . medals of honor." Author's lecture notes. October, 2001.

55   "tried so hard" . . . "live with themselves": Associated Press, December 10, 1984. "Baldwin Executed Proclaiming Innocence."

7. Retribution — "An Eye for an Eye"

65   Statistics concerning numbers of people incarcerated with low IQ: Entzeroth, "Putting the Mentally Retarded Criminal Defendant to Death."

67   "The other kids . . . call Marvin dummy": Rudolf, "Marvin Wilson, Texas Man."

68–69   "An individual . . . and income": Clark, "The Social Psychology of Jury Nullification."

69   "the boys looked like nice young men": Ibid.

8. Deterrence, or a Warning to All

76   "I do not really understand myself . . . any visible physical disorder": Lavergne, "The Legacy of the Texas Tower Sniper."

79   "zero tolerance": Janiskee and Erler, "Crime, Punishment, and Romero."

Murder rate statistics: "Regional and National Murder Rates" fact sheet.

81   Recidivism rates: "State of Recidivism" fact sheet.

11. The Right to Counsel

100   "Why aren't you ready" . . . "trial was scheduled for today?": Lewis, *Gideon's Trumpet.*

102   "The question is very simple . . . the court refused." Ibid.

BIBLIOGRAPHY

United States Constitution

Statutes

18 USCS § 2113: Bank Robbery and Incidental Crimes

Cases

Atkins v. Virginia, 536 U.S. 304 (2002).

Baldwin v. Maggio, 704 F.2d 1325 (1983).

Baldwin v. Maggio, 715 F.2d 152 (1983).

Bradwell v. The State, 83 U.S. 130 (1873).

Brooks v. State, 35 Ohio St. 46 (1878).

Childs v. The State of Nevada, 107 Nev. 584 (1991).

Childs v. The State of Nevada, 109 Nev. 1050 (1993).

Coffin v. U.S., 156 U.S. 432 (1895) (the first mention of "innocent until proven guilty" in United States law).

Commonwealth of Pennsylvania v. Anthony Michael Fowlin, 450 PA Super. 489 (1995).

Commonwealth of Pennsylvania v. Anthony Michael Fowlin, 551 PA 414 (1998).

Gates, Robert, Secretary of Defense v. Haji Bismullah et al., Huzaifa Parhat, et al., 2007 U.S. Briefs 7677, (2008).

Gideon v. Wainwright, 372 U.S. 335 (1963).

Huzaifa Parhat v. Robert Gates, Secretary of Defense, 532 F.3d 835 (2008).

In re Guantanamo Bay Detainee Litigation Jamal Kiyemba, As Next Friend of Abdusabur Doe, et al. v. George W. Bush, 2005 U.S. Distr. Ct., Motions 1509 (July 23, 2008).

Kiyemba v. Obama, 555 F. 3d 1022 (2009).

Kiyemba v. Obama, 561 F. 3d 509 (2009).

Kiyemba v. Obama, 130 S. Ct. 1235 (2010).

Korematsu v. United States, 323 U.S. 214 (1944).

Korematsu v. United States, 584 F.Supp. 1406 (N.D.Cal. Apr. 19, 1984).

Manufacturers and Traders Trust Company v. Maxine A. Given, 2011 U.S. 11th Cir. 14282 (2011).

Mapp v. Ohio, 367 U.S. 643 (1961).

In re Marvin Lee Wilson, 433 F3d 451 (2005).

Marvin Lee Wilson v. The State of Texas, 7 S.W. 3rd 136 (1999).

Miranda v. Arizona, 384 U.S. 436 (1966).

Plessy v. Ferguson, 163 U.S. 537 (1896).

Ramona Trombley, et al. v. National City Bank, 759 F. Supp. 2d 20 (Jan. 11, 2011).

Ramona Trombley, et al., v. National City Bank, 826 F. Supp. 2d 179 (Dec. 1, 2011).

Seixas and Seixas v. Woods, 2 Cai. R. 48 (1804).

State v. A. B. Rhodes, 61 N.C. 453 (1868).

United States v. James Hugh Rogers, 289 F2d 433 (1961).

Legal Briefs

Brief Amicus Curiae, Brennan Center for Justice, *Kiyemba v. Obama, Brennan Center for Justice.*

Brief Amicus Curiae of Fred Korematsu, *Shafiq Rasul v. George W. Bush,* 542 U.S. 466 (2004).

Brief Amicus Curiae of Fred Korematsu, *Rumsfeld v. Padilla,* 542 U.S. 426 (2004).

Books

Chin, Steven A. *When Justice Failed: The Fred Korematsu Story.* Steck-Vaughn, 1992.

Darrow, Clarence. *Attorney for the Damned: Clarence Darrow in the Courtroom.* Edited by Arthur Weinberg. Chicago: University of Chicago Press, 1989.

Davies, W. W. *The Codes of Hammurabi and Moses, with Copius Comments, Index, and Bible References.* New York: Eaton and Mains, 1905.

Dostoevsky, Fyodor. *The House of the Dead.* 1862.

Fletcher, George P. *Basic Concepts of Criminal Law.* Oxford: Oxford University Press, 1998.

Lewis, Anthony. *Gideon's Trumpet.* New York: Vintage Books/Random House, 1964.

Medley, Keith Weldon. *We as Freemen: Plessy v. Ferguson.* Gretna, L.A.: Pelican Publishing Company, 2003.

Packer, Herbert L. "Two Models of the Criminal Process." In *The Limits of the Criminal Sanction.* Stanford: Stanford University Press, 1968.

Persico, Deborah A. *Mapp v. Ohio: Evidence and Search Warrants* Berkeley Heights: Enslow Publishers, 1997.

Articles

Ambrose, Eileen. "Overdraft Angst: Legislation That Would Require Consumers to Opt into Bank Protection Could Curb Stiff Fees." *Baltimore Sun,* September 27, 2009.

"Baldwin Executed Proclaiming Innocence." Associated Press, December 10, 1984.

Bronstein, Phil. "The Man Who Killed Osama bin Laden . . . Is Screwed." *Esquire,* February 11, 2013.

"California Department of Corrections and Rehabilitation: Inmates Sentenced Under the Three Strikes Law." California State Auditor, Report 2009–107.2, May 2010.

Clark, John. "The Social Psychology of Jury Nullification." *Law and Psychology Review* 24 (Spring 2000): 39.

Downey, Mike."Seller Beware in Card Games." *Los Angeles Times,* March 11, 1991.

Eagleman, David. "Sentencing Psychopaths." Baylor College of Medicine's Initiative on Neuroscience and Law, NeuroLaw Blog, October 25, 2010.

Ehlers, Scott, Vincent Schiraldi, and Jason Ziedenberg. "Still Striking Out: Ten Years of California's Three Strikes." *Justice Policy Institute: Policy Report* (2004).

Entzeroth, Lyn. "Putting the Mentally Retarded Criminal Defendant to Death: Charting the Development of a National Consensus to Exempt the Mentally Retarded from the Death Penalty." *Alabama Law Review,* vol. 52 (2001): 911.

Forman, Ross. " '68 Ryan Rookie Card Will Go to Highest Bidder." *USA Today,* June 21, 1991.

Goodno, Naomi Harlin. "Career Criminals Targeted: The Verdict Is In, California's Three Strike Law Proves Effective." *Golden Gate University Law Review,* vol. 37 (Winter 2007): 461.

Janiskee, Brian P., and Edward J. Erler. "Crime, Punishment, and Romero: An Analysis of the Case Against California's Three Strikes Law." *Duquesne Law Review,* vol. 39 (Fall 2000): 42.

Jennings, Peter. *World News Tonight with Peter Jennings.* American Broadcasting Company (ABC News), March 6, 1991.

Jones, Trina. "Inadvertent Disclosure of Privileged Information and the Law of Mistake: Using Substantive Legal Principles to Guide Ethical Decision Making." *Emory Law Journal* 48 (Fall 1999): 1255.

King, Tim. "A Combat Soldier on Death Row?" Salem, Oregon: *Salem-News,* July 27, 2009.

Lavergne, Gary. "The Legacy of the Texas Tower Sniper." *Chronicle of Higher Education* 53, no. 34 (April 27, 2007).

Mandak, Joe. "PTSD Defense Delays Ex-Soldier's Murder Trial." Associated Press, October 10, 2011.

———. "Vet's Double-Murder Trial Set to Open in Pennsylvania." Associated Press, March 18, 2002.

Maslin, Sarah Nir. "Failing to Hit Jackpot, and Hitting Machine Instead." *New York Times,* July 13, 2012.

Mazzetti, Mark, and Helene Cooper. "Detective Work on Courier Led to Breakthrough on Bin Laden." *New York Times,* May 2, 2011.

O'Donnell, Mark. "Chase Overdraft Fee Class Action Settlement." *Top Class Actions,* October 4, 2012.

Redding, Richard. "The Brain-Disordered Defendant: Neuroscience and Legal Insanity in the Twenty-First Century." *American University Law Review,* vol. 56 (October 2006): 51.

Reinmuth, Gary. "Ryan Card Victim Gets Wish." *Chicago Tribune,* July 25, 1993.

Richardson, Clem. "Former NYPD Commissioner Bernard Kerik Says 'Prison Is Like Dying with Your Eyes Open.'" *New York Daily News,* June 13, 2012.

Robinson, Paul, and John Darley. "The Role of Deterrence in the Formulation of Criminal Law Rules: At Its Worst When Doing Its Best." *Georgetown Law Journal,* vol. 91 (2002–3).

Rudolf, John. "Marvin Wilson, Texas Man with 61 I.Q., to Be Executed in Days." Huffington Post, August 3, 2012, updated August 7, 2012.

Simmons, Charlene Wear. "Children of Incarcerated Parents." Prepared at the request of assembly member Kerry Mazzoni, California Research Bureau, March 2000.

Serres, Chris. "Bank Fees Finagles?" *Minneapolis St. Paul Star Tribune,* August 12, 2012.

Shah, Nirvi. "Lawsuit Against Banks for Overdraft Fees Will Go Ahead." *Miami Herald,* March 13, 2010.

Spruill, Willie E., II. "The Exploitation of Bank Charges and Undermining of Consumer Protection: Exploring the Realms of High-to-Low Check Posting." 13 N.C. Banking Institute, vol. 13, p. 433.

Szasz, Thomas S. *The Myth of Mental Illness: Foundations of a Theory of Personal Conduct.* New York: Harper & Row, 1964.

"Targeting the Nation's Leading Killer at a Glance." National Center for Chronic Disease Prevention and Health Promotion, Atlanta, Georgia, 2000.

Verdi, Bob. "Charity Comes Out the Winner in Great Baseball Card Taffy-Pull," *Sporting News,* May 6, 1991.

Vlasic, Mark V. "Assassination and Targeted Killing—A Historical and Post–Bin Laden Legal Analysis." *Georgetown Journal of International Law,* vol. 3 (Winter 2002): 259.

Warden, Rob. "Reflections on Capital Punishment." *Northwestern Journal of Law and Social Policy,* vol. 4 (Fall 2009), p. 329.

Weber, Mark. "The Japanese Camps in California." *Journal for Historical Review* 2, (Spring 1981): 45–58.

West, Paul. "Two Maryland Victims of Banking System Meet with Obama." *Maryland Politics,* October 9, 2009.

Wicker, Tom. "In the Nation, Death Is Different." *New York Times,* May 25, 1982.

Wolff, Nancy, Cynthia Blitz, Jing Shi, Jane Siegel, and Ronet Bachman. "Physical Violence Inside Prisons: Rates of Victimization." *Criminal Justice and Behavior,* vol. 34 (May 2007): 588.

Published Statistics

Correctional Populations in the United States, 2011, U.S. Department of Justice. Each week the Department of Justice, Bureau of Prisons, updates statistics on prison population: www.bop.gov/locations/weekly_report.jsp. For total correctional populations, see www.bjs.gov/index.

International Centre for Prison Studies, an organization in partnership with the University of Essex providing prison research assistance to governments and relevant agencies: www.prisonstudies.org.

"Plea and Charge Bargaining: Research Summary, Bureau of Justice Assistance, U.S. Department of Justice" (prepared by Lindsey Devers, Ph.D.), January 24, 2011.

Autopsy Report

Autopsy of Charles Joseph Whitman, performed at Cook Funeral Home on August 2, 1966. Reproduced from the Collections of the Austin History Center.

Fact Sheets

"Regional and National Murder Rates, 2011–12." Compiled from FBI Uniform Crime Reports by the Death Penalty Information Center (18th Street, NW, Suite 704, Washington D.C.), a national nonprofit organization serving the media and public with analysis and information on issues concerning capital punish-ment.

"State of Recidivism: The Revolving Door of America's Prisons." Pew Center on the States, April 2011.

Interviews

Author interview with Karen Korematsu, January 14, 2014. Ms.

Korematsu corrected factual inaccuracies from Chin's *When Justice Failed: The Fred Korematsu Story* and provided additional facts.

Author correspondence with Nick and Danielle Horner, September 14, 2013, September 22, 2013, October 5, 2013, undated letter from Nick Horner.

INDEX